The Challenge

WILLIAM J. DUPLEY

MARCUS

I BLESS YOU TO MAKE

DISCIPLES

YOURS

William Dupley

The Challenge

WILLIAM J. DUPLEY

Kingdom Heart
—PUBLISHING—
"Inspiring nations to listen to God"

Cataloguing data available from Library and Archives Canada

ISBN: 978-1-4600-1325-0
LSI Edition: 978-1-4600-1326-7
E-book ISBN: 978-1-4600-1327-4
(E-book available from the Kindle Store, KOBO and the iBooks Store)

For more information, please contact:
William Dupley
the.secret.place@cogeco.com
Kingdom Heart Publishing

Cover and illustrations by William Dupley

Kingdom Heart
——PUBLISHING——
"Inspiring nations to listen to God"

Dedication

I dedicate this book to my father, William W. Dupley,
a man committed to kindness.

Contents

Acknowledgements

I t is said that it takes a village to raise a child. I believe it takes a community to write a book as well. I wish to express my gratitude to David Wuyts (UK), Ken Raymar (Canada), Karen Thorneycroft (Canada), Jerry Lenz (USA), Carol Fellman (Canada), Joyce Chadwick (Canada), Jason Major (Canada), Fred Fulford (Canada), Kevin Cormier (Canada), Rob Balamut (Canada), Ilse Desaeger (Belgium), Werner Jöchle (Switzerland), Peter Leishman (Canada), and John Arnott (Australia) for all their advice and help in editing and improving the book. I especially wish to thank Tom Scott (USA), Michael Mckenna (Canada), Karen Tanner (USA), Susan Dupley, and Rev. Al Riemers (Canada), my dear friends, who invested many hours editing the text and recommending changes. Thank you all for your time and friendship.

Introduction

Society is transformed by those who are inspired to change it. In Greenville, a simple challenge from a Pastor inspired a group of men by asking them, "What do you think it would look like if we accomplished what Jesus wanted us to do? How would our world be different if we listened to Him every day and did what He was doing?

This simple word would change these men, and, in just one year, they transformed their entire community; however, each man faced different issues as they considered how to address their Pastor's challenge.

The Challenge describes their journey.

Prologue

That Saturday morning was like any other at the Cozy Corners restaurant. A group of local men met for their monthly men's breakfast in the restaurant's far corner. They were kidding each other about their ability to consume massive quantities of eggs, bacon, and sausages. Conversations usually revolved around topics such as sports, cars, and family.

But not this Saturday morning.

CHAPTER ONE

The Challenge

"I think I'll have the Farmer's breakfast—three eggs, three slices of bacon, sausage, home fries, and pancakes." Jim Michaels always had the Farmer's breakfast. Jim was in his early sixties, slightly balding, with a perpetual grin. Jim was also pushing forty-eight size pants, and although he was not short, he was starting to look like a Roly-poly toy.

Mike exclaimed, "I think I'll have the Healthy Choice today." The rest of the guys began to rib him. Healthy Choice! What happened? Mike Brown always had the Meat Eater's special.

"My doctor says my cholesterol is through the roof, and if I don't change my eating habits, I could have a stroke. I watched my Dad have one of those, and I never want to have to live through that." Mike's words were a reality check on the whole group. We were not getting any younger, and perhaps we had all better look closer at what we ate.

"I still have to keep up my strength," laughed Jim, while the whole crew chuckled. Jim was about 280 pounds, and although at one time he was a star linebacker for our high school football team, well, that was forty years ago, and the 280 pounds of muscle had fallen a little lower in his body.

Every fourth Saturday, we met at Cozy Corners restaurant to chat about cars, catch up on our families, and hear some words of inspiration from Pastor Dave Williams. Our men's group consisted of about a dozen guys. Some of us had known each other since high school. My name is Chris Martin, and I have been attending these breakfasts for years.

Greenville is a small village founded over 200 years ago. It was built by the river, and several mills took advantage of the water-power. Many of the families in our church are descendants of those original Greenville founding families. Their ancestors' graves are in our local cemetery. The cemetery brings awareness that we will eventually pass; however, something is comforting about knowing our heritage. Many of our friends who live in the suburbs don't have this experience. I consider it a precious treasure.

Many of our men's group had moved into our community during a housing boom thirty years ago, and we raised our families here. We are currently experiencing a transformation of our community. The original owners are retiring and choosing to downsize and sell their homes to new younger families. It has been a pleasant change for us; the parks are filled with small kids playing minor-league baseball, and street hockey is in full swing. It is part of life, I guess; the older gives way to the younger. We now have several young men around thirty years old, with young families coming to our monthly breakfast meetings.

We all looked forward to these breakfast meetings. Even the young guys seemed to enjoy the camaraderie of the group. Listening to these younger men brings back memories for us older guys of the challenges most of us had forgotten. Children's problems, the sleepless nights with young babies, the never-ending shortness of money, and the ever-increasing demands on paychecks are all distant memories. I am over sixty, I don't owe anyone anything, and I make more money than I ever did. Listening to the struggles of these young men reminds me of how hard it was just getting started. However, hearing these younger men also reminds me of the dreams and hopes that I had forgotten.

"A Ford 428 Cubic inch will not fit a 57 Chev," erupted Mike. Mike was a mechanic at Greenville Auto, and he was the town expert on everything to do with cars.

"Road & Track magazine said a guy in Ohio did it," declared Jason.

"There is a lot more to engine swaps than just squeezing the engine under the hood, Jason. This guy must have got some special engine swap kit, or he would only have about an inch for the radiator." Mike, of course, was right, and Jason listened.

Jason Anderson is a young man who is a member of one of the founding families of Greenville. His family goes further back than that. I noticed that in our church's graveyard, a gravestone states that one of his ancestors came over on the Mayflower, so he is a member of a founding family of North America. He is about twenty-eight, and he is full of life and fire. He recently told me how he is looking forward to buying a cottage and a Shelby Cobra. Jason hasn't got two cents to rub together. He has student loans, and he has only started to work as a teacher at one of our local schools, but he has dreams. I remember when I had dreams. It seems as you get older, you forget those dreams. Sometimes, because of the reality of life and the shortness of money, those hopes are cut short. Sometimes we just stop dreaming.

Listening to these younger men re-ignites old dreams and passions, which have gone dormant in many of us. At some point, we just settled and decided that this is as good as it is going to get.

Pastor Dave always finishes our breakfast meetings with a word of challenge or encouragement. He's about fifty-five years old and younger than many of us. Dave has curly brown hair and always wears casual dress pants, a T-shirt, and an unbuttoned casual shirt. He likes Hawaiian shirts, although he did not have one on that day. Dave never followed the usual dress code for a Pastor. Dave was a good Pastor, and he did not always stick to the denominational line. He often brought in speakers from other churches and groups that were not affiliated with our denomination. We benefited from those decisions, and we have become much richer spiritually as a result. He looks for people he feels God is moving through, people in whom he senses God's presence is evident. He often says, "Perhaps some of it might rub off on us."

That Saturday, Dave was a lot more somber than usual. He often greets everyone and gives them a slap on the back or at least a big smile. Dave had a way of looking at you, eye-to-eye, face-to-face, that made you feel like you were the only person in the world. You had his full attention. I loved it when he looked at me that way. I met him spirit-to-spirit, and I always felt much better, even though he did not say much. I just felt like my heart was strengthened.

That Saturday was different; Dave seemed much quieter; I could see something was bothering him. My wife says I am oblivious to how other people feel most of the time and that I live in my own little world. I guess that is true. I prefer solitude to being with other people, but I felt empathy each time I looked at Dave. I knew that something was bothering him.

"Dave, are you okay? You seem to be preoccupied this morning."

"Sorry about that, Chris. I just got some heartbreaking news this morning. Cindy has been diagnosed with bowel cancer. It has metastasized, and she has tumours in her liver. She needs to have chemo and surgery. Unfortunately, this type of cancer is very invasive and spreads quickly, and if unchecked, she will likely die within two years."

Dave's words hit me like a sledgehammer. His beloved wife, Cindy, was one of the most generous, kind people I had ever met. She seemed to notice every person who came into the church. She could sense the brokenhearted, the poor, and the downcast within minutes. Unlike some who would say, "Have a nice day," and walk away not wanting to get involved, she would immediately ask the person questions looking for ways to help. Nothing was too small or too big for Cindy. She would rally people in the church and outside the church to come to a person's aid. She was always very respectful of the person and never made a spectacle of them or their needs. She was committed to protecting their dignity.

Now Cindy had cancer. I silently cried out, "Why? Why Lord? Why would someone so kind and generous get this awful disease?" Dave asked me to keep this quiet for the time being. I was not surprised; she once told me she would rather have one person say, "Cancer, leave in the name of Jesus Christ" than listen to hours of prayer that droned on and on and said nothing.

Cindy was not your ordinary Pastors' wife. She was not quiet, submissive, always hiding in her husband's shadow. Cindy was a direct cause-centric person who was passionate about the kingdom and for the oppressed. Although she was born in the early 60s like Dave, she did not act like someone who grew up in the 70s. She always seemed to be a person who would have been more comfortable at Woodstock than on some disco floor.

Joan Baez and Simon Garfunkel, and other musicians of the 60s were always playing in their house. I thought it unusual that she seemed to know all the music I loved yet did not grow up when I did. One day I mentioned this to Dave, and he said Cindy worshipped her brother Andy who was about ten years older than she was. Andy was a star athlete, a real person of action, highly active in civil rights even as a teenager, and very patriotic. In college, he became very concerned about communist expansion. Unlike many of his friends who were happy to be in college to avoid the draft, he wanted to go to Vietnam, and after graduation, he enlisted in the Marines.

Cindy loved him for it. She listened to his music, followed his bands, and watched the evening news every night to find out what was happening in Vietnam. Then in 1968, on a hill at Khe Sanh he died. On February 4, a telegram arrived, notifying the family that Andy had been killed in action. Cindy collapsed on the front porch sobbing and wailing. Nothing could console her. Ever since that time, she seems to keep her brother alive in her heart by listening to his music. Cindy also followed in his footsteps and became an avid activist and protested any perceived injustice. Like Dave, Cindy became a Christian at university, but she never lost her activist heart.

Dave called everyone to attention and said, "I was challenged by the words of Jesus when He said, 'Go into all the world and make disciples, teaching them all that I have commanded you to do.'[i] Although I have read these verses a hundred times, I chose to do a word study on the word 'commanded,' and I discovered something I did not know. The term 'commanded' comes from the Greek verb 'to accomplish.' As I thought about these words of Jesus, they took on an entirely new meaning. Let me read this to you again, 'Go therefore into the whole world and make disciples and teach them all I want them to accomplish.' Adding the words 'to accomplish' changed the whole feel of the verse for me.

"I started to think about how I could accomplish all that He wants me to do instead of thinking about how I should follow all the commandments of Jesus. I did an in-depth Bible study, and I found that there were about eighty-three things Jesus wanted us to accomplish while we are on the earth. However, a vital element of this activity is to look at the result He wanted us to achieve, and then use our minds to think about ways to accomplish this outcome in the sphere of influence where we live. I found this revelation to be refreshing and much different than mindlessly trying to obey a rule. We are not animals that need to be told what to do. We are men and women that God wants to partner with to accomplish what He wants to be done.

"I also read another verse that showed how Jesus accomplished the desires of His Father. It read, 'Very truly I tell you, the Son can do nothing by himself; he can do only what he sees his Father doing, because whatever the Father does the Son also does.'[ii] It was clear from these verses that the key to understanding what we are to accomplish is to listen to our Heavenly Father and do the things He is doing," Dave concluded. "This week, I encourage you to try to do this."

After Dave finished, the men were hushed. It was like something struck all of them simultaneously. There was a sense of eternity in Dave's words that seemed to demand a response. The men were always respectful of Dave when he gave us these short messages; however, I felt that his words seemed to go very deep into the men's hearts this time. They were quiet and contemplative; it was as if Dave's words had shaken them to the core. I felt a deep stirring—not conviction, but more a sense of vision, challenge, and possibility.

As I thought about what Dave said, I could not shake the words he had just told me about Cindy. My heart was upset about the news of her illness. My spirit was angry at the sickness. I cried out, "God, why would you allow this? Why would you allow Cindy to get this awful disease?"

I thought of the Bible story of Jesus sending out the seventy-two disciples without money and telling them to go out and heal the sick and say to them, "The kingdom of God is near you."[iii] I remembered how the seventy-two returned so excited, declaring the great things they had seen done in Jesus' name as they prayed for people. I thought about this, and I felt I had a revelation about what Jesus wanted me to accomplish. I felt like I could be a vessel to impart God's power into Cindy. I thought we should pray for Cindy to be healed of this cancer. I had never felt like this before.

CHAPTER TWO

The Garage

On the way home from our breakfast, I stopped into Greenville Auto to get my oil changed. Paul Robinson owned the garage. Paul was in his late forties. He had blue eyes and a receding hairline, which he always covered up with a baseball cap. Recently he started sporting a short black beard. It made him look quite distinguished.

We only had a few garages in our village, and Paul got much of the local work. He was an honest man and took his job of keeping Greenville vehicles well-maintained exceptionally seriously. Greenville drivers trusted him. He was also an avid car collector, and he always had some sweet classic parked in front of the garage. Today he had a candy-apple-red 1965 Shelby Mustang G.T. 350.

"Awesome car, Paul. When did you get the Mustang?" Paul was behind his desk. His desk was always piled high with papers, invoices, car magazines, and old ashtrays.

"It is sweet, isn't it, Chris? I found it in Arizona and had it shipped up. It has never seen winter, and it is in pristine shape. It drives like a dream."

Paul's Dad had owned the garage before him, and his Dad had

been a two-pack a day smoker who loved his ashtrays. Paul had kept them around even though he didn't smoke and didn't allow smoking in or around the garage. He just liked these antiques. One of them was a stainless-steel ashtray with a large metal model of a plane on the top. Others were solid brass with trucking companies' emblems. One of them had a model of an engine on it. It was like stepping back into history, walking into his office. How times have changed. Only twenty years ago you wouldn't have been able to see in this room for the cigarette smoke.

Paul had grown up in this garage, and from a young age, he was always fascinated with automobiles. His Dad, Jeff Robinson, was a good man, and he built the garage after coming back from serving in the Second World War, but like many of the men of his generation who came back, he did not express his emotions. He would never talk about his experiences in the War. Jeff had volunteered and served as an artillery spotter. He fought through Italy and participated in the liberation of Holland. He fought right through to the end of the War.

Paul often told me he never really knew his Dad. Paul said his Dad was a nice guy, and if he ever had any questions about cars, his Dad was always there with good advice. However, if Paul asked him any questions about the War, life, or relationships, his Dad would clam up and get uptight. He often would retreat into the bottle. There was always a bottle of Scotch in the bottom of his desk drawer.

Dave's Dad likely had Post Traumatic Stress Disorder, but that wasn't something people talked about at that time. Veterans would just go to the Legion and drink to forget. That was the only relief they had. Dave said that the last few years seemed to be worse for his Dad. His memory had started to go, and he didn't remember who Dave was sometimes, but the memories of the War seemed to be there still. At times Jeff had woken up at night from dreams that made him cry. Jeff passed away a couple of years ago, and Dave often speaks of him, but there always seemed to be a longing in his eyes like he wished he had known him better. I could feel the deep ache that weighed on Dave's heart when he talked about his Dad.

Paul always had a smile, even when he had to give you bad news like your shocks are gone or you need new tires. He had earned the trust of the community. Paul was also known for going the extra mile for his customers.

"That was some meeting this morning," Paul said. "I was challenged by Dave. I started reading that list of things Jesus wants us to accomplish. I came across the Scripture, 'Love the Lord your God, with all your heart, soul, mind, and strength.'[iv] I wondered how I could do that.

"I started to list my strengths, and I came up with quite a few. I know I am a good mechanic, and I seem to talk with people easily. I understand that these are strengths. I am a lousy guitar player, and I don't sing very well, even though I do like to do both. I don't think these are my strengths."

Paul was a remarkably humble and honest guy and an excellent musician. We played together at our weekly Thursday night music jam at the church. I told him, "Paul, you are as honest as the day is long. That's a real strength, especially in your business." Paul looked a bit embarrassed at this praise.

"Chris, I treat people the way I want to be treated, but I have started to wonder how I could accomplish loving God with my strengths better. I had some ideas I would like to pass by you, okay?"

I replied, "Sure, shoot. I'm all ears."

"Every few weeks, I get some customer who needs work done on their car, but they can't afford it. Last week, for example, Mary Anders came in; she is the single mother with three boys, you know— David, Andrew, and Joshua. You see them at the church now and then." I remembered seeing them around. "Her brakes were completely shot, and it was going to cost $1000 to fix them, and I knew she couldn't afford it. I talked it over with Mike, my mechanic, and we decided we could do the work and just charge her our cost. We decided to throw in a few extra hours for free. We got the price down to about $500, but it was still too much for her to pay. I'm happy to throw in my time and give up the profit, but I have costs to cover. What do you think we could do about this?"

I thought about it and said, "I saw a restaurant in an inner-city that had two jars full of buttons at the cash register. One jar was full of buttons to buy; the other was full of purchased buttons. The way it worked was when people paid for their lunch, they could buy a button for a dollar and put it into the 'buttons purchased' jar. If someone did not have enough money for lunch, they could take buttons from the 'paid-for' jar and pay for their lunch with them. Perhaps we could do something like that here. We just offer buttons for five or ten dollars to people who get their car fixed here, and ask them if they want to buy a button to help others in our town that can't afford to get their car fixed. Then when someone like Mary comes in, you can take buttons from the prepaid jar and cover some or all of her bill."

Paul loved it. We called around to the other members of our men's group and explained the idea. They all chipped in, and soon we had over $1000 of buttons in the jar. Paul called Mary and asked if she could afford $200 to fix her car. Paul still repaired the vehicle at cost, but he could pay his mechanic and some of the parts with the buttons from the button jar.

Restaurants in town heard about the idea, and soon they added button jars as well. The button jars filled rapidly.

All this generosity came forth because one mechanic just asked how he could love the Lord with his strength.

CHAPTER THREE

The Prayer

W hen I got home from breakfast, I talked with my wife, Linda, about Cindy's condition. Linda told me Cindy had already told her, but she could not share it with anyone. Cindy had become a very close friend of Linda, and together they had worked on many of Cindy's projects to bring practical help to those in need. Linda said, "What can we do?" I told her what Pastor Dave had told us that morning about purposely trying to accomplish what Jesus wants us to achieve, and listen to our Heavenly Father and do the things He is doing. I told her that I thought Jesus wanted us to impart God's power to heal Cindy of this cancer in her body.

Linda was a bit shocked at the statement. She said, "Chris, we don't heal the sick, Jesus does. How can you say Jesus wants us to impart God's power to heal Cindy of this cancer?"

I told her about the story in the Bible of Jesus sending out the seventy-two disciples and how they came back rejoicing about the fantastic things they had done in His name. "He told them, 'Heal the sick who are there and tell them the kingdom of God is near.' I think this is what He wants us to accomplish. He wants us to heal the sick. He said, 'Whatever you ask in My name, I will do it.'ᵛ He also said that 'we will do greater things than He did.'" I told her I felt God had given me a revelation or a word or something like that. I didn't know what to call it. I just felt like we could do this. I felt faith come into my heart. I thought we could impart God's healing power into Cindy, and that would heal her.

Linda sat in silence, "Heal the sick. I never thought of this as something we do. I know that Jesus wants us to love our neighbor as ourselves, I know He wants us to accomplish this, but heal the sick! That seems too hard."

"I know, Linda. I can hardly believe the thought came into my head. I didn't expect it, and I have no idea how to do this."

Linda replied, "I pray for the sick all the time. Our prayer group has many people on its prayer list that need healing. However, I never thought of it as us healing the sick. I think of it as us asking Jesus to heal the sick."

"Linda, I don't think Jesus is implying that the disciples had the power in themselves to heal the sick, but they were a conduit for God's power to flow through them when they prayed for healing in Jesus' name. I think God just wants us to be that conduit. The reality, however, is we have to choose to be that conduit. We have to go and lay hands on Cindy and ask for God's power to flow into Cindy and heal her. I know Cindy doesn't want many people to know, but I think we should go over and try to heal her. I know that this sounds presumptuous or even ridiculous since we are just ordinary people, but at least we can try. After all, Jesus told us to love our neighbours as ourselves. We want healing when we are sick. I think we should want the same for our neighbours as well."

"Okay, let's go and see Cindy," replied Linda.

I called Dave and asked if we could come over and see Cindy. He said, "Great. The coffee is on." Dave and Cindy lived on the north side of Greenville. They had a lovely place that backed onto the river. They had many church events in their backyard, and we all loved their hospitality.

As we drove over, I thought, "What am I doing? I am nobody; I am just a business guy; I am nothing special. Who am I to think that God would heal the sick through me? God uses specially anointed people to do stuff like this." I felt both anxiety and stupid all at the same time. Dave met us at the door, and I told him I had thought about what he said this morning, and I felt we should come over and impart God's healing power into Cindy. He was surprised. I told him of the seventy-two disciples' story and that they were told to heal the sick.

Cindy overheard us talking and asked us to come on in. "I would love to be healed." She told us of the bowel cancer diagnosis and the tumours in her liver. I could see in her eyes a combination of despair and hope. She was a great woman of faith, but even Jesus wept in the garden when He considered the cross. I could not help but feel she was feeling something similar to that. I felt afraid again. I felt I had no faith. Then all of a sudden, I felt a gush of compassion. I was in tears as I thought about my dear friend suffering from this awful disease. I wanted to do something; I had the strangest set of conflicting feelings.

We were not sure how to impart healing power. We didn't know how to go about it, so we just started by laying hands on Cindy, and as we did, we felt God's presence come over us. It felt like a tingling sensation flowing over our heads, arms, and hands. Instead of praying, we just spoke to cancer and said: "In the name of Jesus, cancer, we command you to leave Cindy, and we loose healing into Cindy's bowels and liver. Tumours, we command you to shrink and leave Cindy's liver. Amen!"

As we prayed, we felt waves of power flowing over us, and we continued to lay hands on her for a while. These waves of power felt like waves on a beach. They grew in intensity, then diminished, then they came again. I felt like we were imparting energy into her body. I felt like we were a hose or a pipe that was directing the flow of God's anointing into Cindy. This was unlike any prayer we had prayed before. We felt we were actively involved in the healing process. We did not see anything, but we just kept imparting God's anointing, and we did not leave until the sense of His presence subsided.

Cindy began to weep. She broke down and sobbed, "I have been very reluctant to share my situation with the church. I can't stand peoples' pity and how they look at you when you're sick. It robs my faith. I felt God's power come over me when you prayed. I know something happened today. Please come and pray with me like that until the cancer is gone?" We wept with her. It was the first time I'd ever seen her so transparent, so vulnerable. Linda and I said, "We will come over every week and impart God's presence and command the tumours to go."

Linda asked if she could share Cindy's situation with her prayer group. Cindy said, "Sure, but don't use my name. I don't want people to know in the church. As I said, I couldn't take any pity from well-meaning people who say, 'I'm so sorry to hear about your illness.' I just need people of faith to spark life into my body."

As we left their home, I said to Linda, "That wasn't so hard. I wonder how long it will be before we hear that she is healed."

CHAPTER FOUR

Town Hall

Jason Anderson recently started teaching high school at Greenville High. Jason was a tall, lanky guy about six foot four, about one hundred and eighty pounds, and like most guys his age, he had short-cropped blond hair and always wore a baseball cap. It was hard to tell him apart from the kids he was teaching. I think his look and his love for video games made him more popular with the students. Although this was his first teaching assignment, it was clear he was a natural-born teacher and was already proving to be a real asset to our community.

Jason was not new to our community. I had seen him play baseball many times when he was growing up. Jason was a farm boy, but farming did not hold any interest for him. He loved to teach and specialized in math and sciences, obtained an undergraduate degree in mathematics and chemistry, and had a Master's degree in history and political science. We were fortunate that he decided to come back to Greenville and be a teacher.

His students loved him, partly because he wasn't much older than they were and partly because his classes were always fascinating. When he taught science, he did not just share facts. He would teach them the history of the scientists who made crucial discoveries. He shared fascinating facts about the political world they lived in and the challenges they had to overcome to develop their innovations. He related science to real issues, such as the impact of chemicals on our local farms and North America's food production capability. He explained the effect of heavy metals from old manufacturing plants on our water supply system. His classes produced more ecology-minded people than any teacher or program in our county.

Jason also had some of the most exciting insights at our breakfast meetings. He would tell us historical truth that none of us were aware of, and I enjoyed his company. One morning we ran into each other while getting a coffee on our way to work, and stopped for a quick chat. He, too, brought up Dave's talk and said, "I thought a lot about Dave's challenge. I thought about that Scripture about loving the Lord with your heart, soul, strength, and mind." I was surprised that the same Scripture that caught Jason's eyes was the same one that challenged Paul. I wondered if God was talking to all of us about the same thing.

Jason continued, "I asked myself, 'How do I love God with my mind?' I love to study, and teaching is my passion. I seem to have success with my students, but I feel I could do more. I wake up in the morning with ideas about improving our community and how to attract business to our community. I've noticed that many of my students leave Greenville after graduating to get work. I have also noticed that our manufacturing companies have closed. I have seen four of our main employers leave our area in just my lifetime. It bothers me. Greenville is a great community to raise a family. I have wondered if I could do something about this. I had a few ideas that I wanted to share with our Town Council, but I don't know anyone. Could you help me?"

"Julie Walker is on the Town Council. Her husband, Ryan, comes to the breakfast meetings. I am sure he could arrange for you to talk to her. Have you ever thought of running for political office, perhaps be a Councilperson yourself? You understand politics, and you have a heart for our community. Some fresh blood would be helpful in our political scene. Most of the men and women on the Council have been in those jobs for years. They've done a good job, but we need an infusion of new thought."

"I have never thought of that," Jason replied. "I believe I could provide some good ideas. Would that be accomplishing something God wants me to do?"

"Jason, the Lord, puts us on the earth to manage this world. The Bible calls us to subdue the earth.[vi] It was the first mandate that God gave Adam and Eve. The apostle Paul talked a lot about rulers and how God establishes rulers to rule communities and countries. We are encouraged to pray for those in authority.[vii] The problem is, some people going into politics are going into it for personal gain, or worse, because they love power. We have seen this for years on the world stage.

"Jesus talks a lot about the actual characteristics of a good leader. He summed it up in a few words. He said, 'Whoever wants to be great amongst you must become a servant of all.'[viii] Jesus even demonstrated this by washing the feet of His disciples. Only a slave did that work in His time.

"Community leaders who see themselves as servants to their community and demonstrate a servant's heart can change a nation. Robert Greenleaf wrote a very famous business book a few years ago called *Servant Leadership*. It illustrates the servant leadership model."

Jason pondered these thoughts and declared, "I can do this. I understand political systems. I have many ideas on how to improve our community's commerce, and even how we could attract some manufacturing plants back to our community. I also feel that the Lord is encouraging me to do this. It feels a bit daunting, but I have peace in my heart, and I'm excited about it."

I said, "I suggest you create a report on our current situation in Greenville. Consider employment losses, changes in demographics, and forecast the current changes on both if left unchecked. Also, create a portfolio of ideas and how our situation could be reversed. I'll review it with you and then arrange for you to meet with Julie to discuss your ideas and observations. I have known Julie and Ryan for years. They are both the salt of the earth, and they would love to hear your thoughts. Jason, you started our discussion with how you could love the Lord with your mind. You have just done that. Because of your ideas, thoughts, and passion, you will likely change our community. You will create work, and provide a reason for our children to stay in Greenville. You are a great gift to our community. I'm looking forward to working with you on this."

It is incredible what can happen in a coffee lineup on a Tuesday morning.

CHAPTER FIVE

The Farmer's Market

Saturday morning is a busy day in Greenville. It is our Farmers' Market day. Farmers and other small businesses bring their wares, crafts, etc., to the centre of town to the central parking area beside the Town Hall and set up their stalls. The produce is always fresh, and it is a highlight for our community.

Joseph and Maria Rodriguez immigrated to our area from Mexico about twenty years ago. Joseph had started to come to Greenville as a migrant worker when he was a teenager, and for over ten years, he worked on Richard and Nancy Brown's farm. Richard was part of our men's group. Joseph wanted to develop his agricultural skills, and he also wanted to immigrate to our country.

Richard took a keen interest in Joseph and spent a lot of time teaching him how to farm. Joseph was a quick learner, and soon Richard gave him oversight responsibilities for the farm. He also helped him get his high school diploma and enrolled him in a local online agricultural college. Joseph threw his whole heart into this activity and, although it was difficult, since English was not his first language, he did persevere.

Richard spent a lot of time with him coaching him. After eight years of online school, Joseph finished with a Bachelor of Science in agricultural systems management with a minor in Agribusiness. One year later, Joseph and his wife Maria applied for citizenship and were accepted. Over the following years, they rented land and eventually purchased a farm, and have built a prosperous mixed vegetable farm specializing in organic crops. The produce is always in high demand at our Farmers' Market, and he also sells to local specialty restaurants that want natural products.

Joseph and Maria now have ten migrant workers working for them on their farm. He teaches them how to be farmers and assists them through the immigration process. Joseph is also a member of our men's breakfast meeting. I stopped by his stall at the market, and he came running up to me with a grin from ear to ear.

"Chris, you never guess what I found on the farm the other day. I was out in the back forty clearing junk out of one of the old machine sheds, and I uncovered a 1948 Ford pickup truck."

"Joseph, that's a real find. That pickup truck was one of the first civilian vehicles made after WWII. What shape is it in?"

"Chris, the body integrity looks good, but it is pretty clear it hasn't been running for a long time. I wonder why it was covered in all that stuff?"

"That's not uncommon, Joseph. Farmers in the area rarely get rid of old things. They just put old vehicles out in the field to rust away just in case they might need a spare part or something. I expect your previous owner just forgot about it. It looks like you have a great restoration project."

"I am sure it is, Chris, but I don't have the time to work on it. The farm takes up my whole day."

"Joseph, you might be surprised. The car restoration bug seems to bite everybody in the men's group at some point."

"Chris, speaking about the men's group, Dave's message got me thinking. I started to examine my life. I am so busy running the farm. I had never thought about his challenge, but all of a sudden, I feel a need to act."

I was surprised by Joseph's transparency. Joseph was already doing many of the things we had discussed. He was honest, loved his family, developed others, and his products were of the highest quality.

However, I felt I wanted to say something useful to him. I felt a deep desire to have a word to encourage him, and this was a new feeling for me that I could not shake. I prayed in my heart and asked the Lord what He would like to say to Joseph; immediately, the following stream of thoughts came to me.

"Son,

"Tell Joseph that I am happy with him. Tell him I love how he serves those who work for him and how his investment will bear great fruit in their lives, their family's lives, and their country. He is a messenger of life and hope to these people, and as a result, he has provided light to an entire community in Mexico. It is here he can start to accomplish more.

"His community back in Mexico is poor, and most men have to leave for months at a time to get work. The agricultural practices in his community are lacking. The land is fertile and, with irrigation, they could produce excellent crops, yet the people don't know how. He can teach them. He can provide leadership and teach them how to manage and plan their crops.

"He can show them how to grow their crops and set up Agribusinesses to produce fruit and food products with a higher value. He can do all these things. Son, tell Joseph this."

I told Joseph what I felt the Lord had said to me. His eyes started to sparkle. He mused, "I could do that. I know how, and perhaps I could start with the workers I have now. Although some want to come to this country, most don't like the weather and would prefer to live in Mexico where it is warm. I will discuss this with them and see if any want to do this. Thanks, Chris."

There is a proverb that says, "As iron sharpens iron so one person sharpens another."[ix] I think about that proverb when I think about our men's group. We sharpen each other; we help each other get ideas that increase our clarity and focus.

CHAPTER SIX

Zahra

"I think I'll have the Farmer's breakfast," Jim said as if that was a surprise.

A month had passed, and we were back at the Cozy Corner restaurant for our monthly Greenville Community Church men's breakfast. There was an air of excitement; everyone was talking and was glad to be there. The entire scene reminded me of a team, perhaps a hockey team that had just won their final match. They were celebrating. It was curious to watch; both old and young were telling each other about things they had done this month to show how they were doing the things Jesus wanted them to accomplish.

Jim even said he took out his neighbour's trash and cut his lawn the other day. He said it seemed like an easy way to love his neighbour as himself. The air was alive with stories, and I was amazed. This morning was not your average breakfast meeting. It reminded me of the excitement the seventy-two disciples had when they returned to Jesus after they went out and healed the sick and cast out demons.

Dave was also very up; he was not deep in thought like last month. Linda and I had seen Cindy every week since the last time we met. She had surgery, and they removed cancer from her bowel, but the tumours in her liver were still there. Her spirit, however, was lifted, and although she was still ill, her heart was happy, and so was Dave.

Mohammed was one of the first to speak up. Mohammed was a new member of our group. He and his wife Zahra and their two daughters had started to come to the church several months ago. They were Syrian refugees that the church had sponsored about a year ago. When they first came, they spoke little English.

Mohammed and Zahra Abu were well-educated. Mohammed was an engineer, and Zahra was a respiratory technician back in Syria. The Syrian Civil War had utterly destroyed their lives. Their home and town were bombed. The hospital where Zahra worked and the manufacturing plant where Mohammed was employed were both destroyed. Mohammed once confided in me that they had a beautiful life in Syria; they had a lovely home and a servant who looked after their kids and prepared their meals. Their girls were in a private school. Then, in one day, their entire life was destroyed, and they were homeless, out of work, and scrambling to stay alive. He was grateful to our country for taking them in.

Mohammed and Zahra were doing well learning English, and they were faithful Muslims, though Mohammed once told me his faith was deeply shaken when all this happened to him. They had become friends with Sharon and Daniel Miller. Daniel was a long-time member of our men's group. Daniel's father and his father before him were well known in our community, and their store, Miller's Hardware, was a fixture in our town. They provided almost everything we needed to fix our homes and farms. They also specialized in free advice. For nearly one hundred years, town folks knew that if you did not know how to do something around your house, like fix a faucet or repair your roof, you could ask the Millers, and they would help you. Before we had Google, we had the Millers. A couple of months ago, Sharon had told my wife Linda the most remarkable story. She said Zahra came to see her and said she had a dream. She said, "Jesus came and sat on my bed. I was sick, and Jesus healed me." She asked Sharon, "Why do I have to be a Muslim?"

Sharon did not know what to say. She did not want to offend her or force her faith in Christ on Zahra, but she saw this as a situation where she could just answer her question.

Sharon said, "Zahra, you don't have to be a Muslim. Your Heavenly Father gave you the freedom of choice. God wants us to be free to choose. However, choices come with responsibilities. All of us will one day face the Lord and give an account of our lives. We will provide a report of our choices."

Sharon continued, "I have not always made the right decisions. My life was pretty wild when I was younger, and I'm ashamed of many things I did. I lived in fear and shame from my lies and sins before accepting Christ as my Saviour. I became a Christian in University and accepted Jesus as my Saviour on a street corner. A man was preaching and declaring Jesus would forgive me if I would just choose to receive God's gift of salvation, made possible through the love of his Son Jesus Christ. He said to me Jesus took my sin on His body when He died on a cross. He told me that Jesus would wash away my shame and forgive me. That day I chose to be a Christian, and God's forgiveness filled my heart. I felt forgiven, and the guilt left me.

"Over the next few months, I learned about my Heavenly Father and how much He loved me. I learned how to hear His voice, and to this day, I talk with Him, and He talks to me. Every day I write my conversations with Him in my journal. I'm not afraid of God. He is not a big cop in the sky with a big stick waiting to whack me if I do something wrong. I know Him as my Heavenly Dad, who just loves me as his little girl. I know He longs to have an intimate personal relationship with me. Zahra, you can choose to have this relationship as well."

Zahra's eyes welled up with tears as Sharon related her experience. She said, "I have never heard anyone tell me this. I've never heard of anyone who would call God their Dad or even say they talked with Him, and He talked back to them. I want this. I want what you have."

Sharon said, "Zahra, it's simple. You just start by acknowledging your need before the Lord. Tell Him you no longer want to be lord of your life and that you want Him to be Lord of your life. Next, accept that Jesus is the Son of God who died on a cross to pay for your sins and mistakes that you have made. Lastly, receive the Holy Spirit. He will lead you into all truth.

"We Christians accept that we are weak, and need God's strength to live. We admit we have made mistakes and will continue to make mistakes, but God's Son's sacrifice gives us access to our Heavenly Father. As a result, we can boldly enter into our Heavenly Father's throne room, jump up on His lap, and get a great big kiss from our Heavenly Dad."

Zahra wept, "I want this, I accept this," and at that moment, she became a Christian. Her face was filled with joy. Sharon laid her hands on her, and she was filled with the presence of God. Zahra wept again, but this time it was not tears of sorrow but tears of joy and happiness. Her face began to radiate with the broadest smile. "I have to go home and tell Mohammed." As Zahra left, Sharon was more surprised than anyone that this had just happened. She did not try to lead someone to Jesus. She just told her own story, and Zahra had just wanted to accept the Lord.

Zahra went home and told Mohammed all that had happened. At first, he was angry. He felt betrayed. Mohammed had always been a good Muslim. He kept to his ritual of daily prayers, and although he did not embrace the extreme teaching of some of the Imams he grew up with, he was a firm believer in Allah. However, he could not shake the look on Zahra's face.

She just seemed to shine. Her eyes were alive with life, she was smiling from ear to ear, and she was singing. She gave him the biggest hug and kiss that Mohammed had ever received; she was just bubbling with love. He could not escape this fact, although, on the outside, his face was stern. On the inside, Mohammed could feel tears rolling up. He could see something had happened to his wife. It looked like the weight of the world had been lifted off her heart.

She was like a little girl without a care in the world. The more Mohammed tried to stay hard, the more he felt broken inside. He kept up his stern face for the rest of the day; however, when he went for his nightly prayers, he told me he suddenly could smell fresh bread.

He opened his eyes to check the oven. Zahra had not made bread. Again, he went back to his prayer rug, and as he knelt, he smelled fresh bread, and then he heard a quiet voice in his mind say, "I am the bread of life."

Mohammed had never experienced anything like this. He asked the voice, "Who are you?" The quiet voice said, "Jesus." These words visibly shook Mohammed. In his thirty-five years of kneeling and praying, he had never heard a voice in his head. He wondered if he was going mad. He got up from his prayer rug and went to the computer and typed, "Jesus bread of life." To his amazement, Google came back with the Bible reference of John 6:35 "Then Jesus declared, 'I am the bread of life. Whoever comes to me will never go hungry, and whoever believes in me will never be thirsty.'"

Tears began to well up in his eyes. For the last two years, his number one prayer to Allah was, "Please help me to provide for my family." He feared he would not have food and shelter. He was thankful that the Christian church had sponsored him and his family. He considered this to be an answer to his prayers. Now he felt profoundly challenged. Perhaps it was Jesus who had answered his prayers.

Mohammed dropped to his knees and cried out, "Jesus, I don't know anything about You, but You have told me You are the bread of life. My wonderful wife seems to have had some encounters with You as well. I ask You to help me if You are the true God." At once, the presence of God overwhelmed him, and Mohammed began to sob as he felt wave after wave of God's presence rolling over him. He explained, "It was like I was on a beach, and wave after wave of love just rolled over me. I could feel it on my head and my arms and my shoulders. I felt like every hair on my arms and head was standing on end; it was so overwhelming. I did not want it to stop. I kept asking, "More, please, more, please, don't stop."

That night both Mohammed and Zahra told me that they had had the best sleep in years. God had come into their lives.

CHAPTER SEVEN

The Internet

Mohammed spoke up and said, "I was deeply challenged by what Dave said last month." He told us he had looked up all eighty-three things Jesus wanted us to accomplish on the list that David had given us. He said, "I read that the greatest commandment was I should love the Lord my God with all my heart, with all my soul, all my strength, and all my mind."ˣ I realized that it was a very encompassing list—heart, soul, strength, and mind. As I considered this, I thought about how I could love the Lord with all my heart.

"Ideas seemed to come to my mind. I thought I could love the Lord in all my actions if I changed how I talked to people, and how I interacted with my wife and my kids. If I just responded with kindness when I was in a store or driving to work, I could achieve this goal. I realized the Lord was speaking to me and that I was hearing what the Father wanted me to do.

"I then began to think about my soul. I understand that my soul has to do with my emotions, my feelings, my heart's desires. I felt if I could change what I desired, I could achieve this outcome. I felt challenged. I've never been someone who wanted power, position, or fame, but I've always had a lot of desire for sex. It's been a challenge for me all of my life.

"My wife and I have a good sexual relationship, but I often want more, and I find myself looking at other women. In Syria, most of the women wear burqas. However, that didn't stop my imagination from wondering what was under those black robes. Here I found that the Internet has a lot to look at and, although I try not to look at it, I find myself drawn to specific websites. I know it is wrong, but I still seem to give in to it."

The group was dumbfounded. No one had ever spoken so openly about their problems, much less a problem with pornography. Mark King, who had recently separated from his wife, Sarah, said, "I have the same problem as well. I would often go down to my den after having sex with my wife and look at porn. It became an all-consuming habit.

"I started to ask my wife to do the things I saw on the sites, but she refused. I would later retreat to my private world of porn queens, and soon I was not paying any attention to Sarah. She knew what I was doing, and she didn't get on my back about it. If she had, I would have just gone on the defensive. One day she said, 'Mark, I feel like you have a mistress. I know you're not cheating on me with a physical woman, but I feel the presence of those girls you look at on the web are in my bed when I lay with you. I know that sounds weird, but it's like they are there with us, and I don't want to be transparent and open with you as a result. Could you please stop looking at those sites?'

"I said I was sorry and told her I would stop, but I didn't. I just got sneaky about it. Unfortunately, she knew, and a few months later, she confronted me again and said: 'Mark, I don't feel you have stopped looking at those sites, and I feel you're lying to me. Is this true?' At first, I tried to blow it off, but I felt convicted and said, 'I am still looking at the sites.' The truth was, I was addicted. I was finding it harder and harder to get aroused, so I started to take Viagra, which led to some very embarrassing situations."

There was a chuckle around the table. "I started to go to a counsellor with Sarah, but by this time, I had eroded her trust, and I no longer seemed to be able to control myself. Our family computer was now full of porn sites, and my kids had seen some of them. Finally, Sarah said, 'I can't live like this. I can't have our kids exposed to this and I need to leave you.'

"I was shocked that afternoon when she left with the kids. That evening as I sat alone in my house with my porn sites, I thought, 'What have I done? I have destroyed my life.' If only I had taken seriously the words Jesus said, to love the Lord with my soul, I would not be in this mess. I don't know what to do."

Several of the men came around him. They confided they were having problems in this area as well. As a group, they confessed their faults to one another and could not hold back their tears. As they wiped away their tears, they said, "Let's hold each other accountable." They said, "Let's ask each other each time we see each other if we had the victory in this area, and if not, why not." They prayed for each other and committed to being available to one another at any time, day or night, to help one another when they felt tempted to look. They also determined to wipe the history and favourite sites from their computers.

This was not your average breakfast meeting.

CHAPTER EIGHT

Loneliness

Every Thursday night, a group of us from the community met at Greenville Community Church to jam and play music. We have several guitar players as well as other musicians. Andrew plays the mandolin, Sharon plays the keyboard, Debbie plays the ukulele, and Jim wails on the banjo. We also have several singers. For two hours or more, we play all kinds of songs, from Rock to Gospel.

Jeff Masters is the brainchild of this little group. Jeff is a retired corporate executive and an avid musician. He has done a fantastic job leading the group and creating a music book that we can all play. He works hard to involve everyone in the group. I have played with other groups, and often it feels like the leader just wants the group to be a backup band for them. Jeff is not like that. He is supportive of each member and is always open to ideas and musical correction. It has been an absolute pleasure to play with him and the band.

Most people who attend do not go to our church, but they just love to get together to play music. Occasionally, we get asked to play community social events, but we only play for ourselves for the most part. There is excellent camaraderie within the band, and the door is always open to new members.

"I look forward to coming to this meeting every week," said Andrew. Andrew was about my age, and he had just started coming to the band meetings. "Ever since my wife passed away, it has been tough. I have real bouts of loneliness. Annie and I were married for forty-two years. When she passed away from cancer last year, I thought my life was over. I retired only a year before, and I thought that now we could travel and enjoy our lives, but then, in less than a year, she was gone. This group has saved me. I always played music with Annie, and we sang all the time on road trips. I thought that area of my life was over, but this little group has rescued me from the tyranny of an empty house." I was taken aback by Andrew's honesty, and it caught me off guard that he saw this little music group as a saving grace. It got me thinking that I bet there are a lot of people like Andrew. Men and women who had lost partners through death or divorce who felt the same way.

The next day I was reading my email, and a LinkedIn message came in that said: "Loneliness is Everybody's Business." The article focused on a young man who had accepted a new job in a town away from home and felt lonely. I read that loneliness was a significant problem in our society. Mother Teresa said, "The most terrible poverty is loneliness and the feeling of being unloved."

Pearl S. Buck said, "The person who tries to live alone will not succeed as a human being. His heart withers if it does not answer another heart. His mind shrinks away if he hears only the echoes of his thoughts and finds no other inspiration." I read other articles that conveyed that loneliness was becoming a chronic problem, even in the workplace. People communicate only using email and messaging, and often go all day without interacting with another person face-to-face.

I remembered a Scripture that told us not to neglect the gathering together of ourselves, which is the custom of some.[xi] We need each other. The Bible says that we are all parts of a Body, and as a physical body, we need all of the elements to work correctly.[xii] We all have a role to play, and we need each other. Now that does not mean we all have to go to church at the same time. Everyone meeting at 10:30 Sunday morning for one-and-a-half hours, while not talking with each other will not accomplish healthy relationships. To achieve this, we needed to step out of our protected little world and interact with others on a face-to-face basis. The concept challenged me that we were designed to be one Body, and I felt, "Everyone needs to feel like they belong somewhere, even in a small music band."

I remembered when Linda and I were trying to find a new church home when we first moved to Greenville. We visited several churches before coming to the Greenville community. I remembered how uncomfortable we felt in some of the churches. We were often ignored. People sometimes would arrive at the church, talk with each other, have a great time, and never said hi or welcomed us. We usually just wanted to leave because we felt like we didn't belong there.

After visiting several churches, we found this was typical behavior. I mused that if we, as believers, felt uncomfortable, how much more would people who do not have a church background feel. I can assume that people would avoid that discomfort like the plague. The whole experience made me start to look at our church with different eyes. I thought, "We must not be like that. We have to seek out the newcomers and make sure they feel welcomed."

Through all these experiences, I hungered for and felt that the Lord wanted us to develop deep, genuine relationships. In our little town, it's easy not to get involved. We meet people at church and at the market; we wave and show genuine pleasure when we meet and greet one another, but it rarely goes beyond that point. It takes an effort to care, to listen, to feel empathy. One person once told us on Facebook how their loneliness was all-encompassing. They thought that if they died, they would never be missed. They had been considering suicide but did not know how to do it. It is an all too common story. We have more methods of communication than we have ever had, yet we seem to communicate less.

It takes an effort to listen, give focused attention, invite people to come to our homes, and practice hospitality. There seems to be a fear developing in our town recently. People are suspicious of others who are too friendly; perhaps it's because so many have been burned by people who seem to show friendship but just want to sell them something, expand their network, or become part of their pyramid scheme.

These types of activities have done significant damage to our church and have caused many not to trust one another. This behaviour has to change. We need to invite people to dinner or get together with no other goal than to build relationships and break down these fears. I decided to discuss my feelings and observations with Dave.

"Dave, I feel challenged that we need to address the chronic loneliness problem that is coming over our society." Dave and I often met for coffee just to catch up and chat. "Linda and I play at the Thursday night Jam session in the church, and one of the members told me how the Jam session had saved him from loneliness." I related the other experiences that I had been thinking about and said, "I think that the Lord wants us to consider new ways to utilize our church building, and how we respond to visitors."

I suggested changing the church from being just a meeting place for believers on Sunday, to a community meeting facility for music jams, hobby nights, painting classes, and book clubs. The possibilities were endless. "Think about it. The church is empty most of the time; we could be a centre that facilitates people getting together, and help break this curse of loneliness in our community. In this way, we can help be a light in our community and perhaps be available to those who have given up hope." I further related my experiences with visiting other churches and being ignored. I told him about a friend of mine, named Oscar, at another church who searched for new people and endeavored to make them feel welcome.

Dave said, "Chris, we already have greeters who have a job of welcoming people. How is this different?"

"Dave, Oscar did not just welcome them and then go on to the next person. He would give direct eye contact and ask them where they were from, and about their family. Oscar would introduce them to other people. If he found out they were new in town, he would give them a card with his name on it, and tell them to call him if they needed help finding things or needed some help getting involved in the community or the church. Oscar became the go-to resource for people to call. Everybody knew Oscar."

Dave responded, "That is a great idea, Chris. Who do you think can do this?"

I felt a twinge of conviction, excitement, and challenge all at the same time. I felt like it was Jesus standing there and asking me to do this. I said, "Chris, I think Linda and I could this."

"Great! The job is yours," Dave responded.

"Chris, did you know that the early Church did not meet in a building?" asked Dave. "They met in homes. When Jesus said, 'I will build my Church,' He never intended it to be a bunch of buildings. He never said, 'I will build my synagogue or my temple.' The early Church met in homes around a meal and shared their faith. The apostle Paul started churches this way. Unfortunately, over the years, people have interpreted the word 'church' to mean 'a building.' I think we need to go back to the original concept. Chris, I have an idea that we might want to consider. What do you think if we, as members of the church, start facilitating a potluck dinner in our homes for the people who attend our church? We could invite some of the new people to attend. I am confident this would help new visitors to plug into church life quickly, and together we could minister to their needs and get to know them."

I felt my heart leap at this idea. I could hardly contain my excitement. "Dave, I think Linda and I would love to do this. I will check with her, but I'm pretty sure she will feel as excited about it as I do."

"Great, let me know what she says," Dave replied.

The Lord will often give us eyes to see the need and then offer us the opportunity to fill the need.

CHAPTER NINE

Football

Football is a big deal in our town, and we show our support for our hometown team. Friday night games are a town highlight, and many families make a tailgate picnic out of the event. It is an excellent time to come together as a community. I was never a great sport's guy. I was too small, and frankly, I was more interested in technology when I was in high school than sports, but now I attend every game.

I saw Jason standing with several of the kids and called out, "Jason, it looks like we are going to do well this year. That new quarterback is doing an amazing job."

Jason replied, "Wesley Smith is doing a remarkable job. The team respects him, and although he is younger than some of the team members and certainly not as boisterous, the team has voted him to be the captain."

"That is some achievement for a younger player, isn't it?" I responded.

"It is unusual," declared Jason. "Usually, the most senior player gets voted to be captain," he went on to say. "There are different types of players on a football team. You have guys who can be very loud without saying a lot, others who only speak up when they have something important to say, and then you have a very few who don't say that much but lead by example. Wesley is like that. He continually leads by example. If the coach is riding a team member hard and the team member doesn't want to say anything, Wesley often goes to the coach and respectfully lets him know. He also ensures the team has the best equipment, and he is always encouraging other members. Lastly, Wesley doesn't hog the ball. He involves the other team members. He is a real team player."

"That's remarkable Jason. How come you know so much about this guy?"

"Chris, I am his homeroom teacher, and I have watched him over the last couple of years, and I have consistently seen these behaviours. You know he won't tell you this stuff. He is a humble guy."

"Was he always like this?" I asked.

"Well, it all started when we had a motivational speaker who was a Christian come to the school a couple of years ago and give a talk at an assembly about how an individual can make a difference. Of course, this guy could not use Christian words or preach, as that would not be allowed in the school, but he delivered an amazing challenge to the kids about making a difference. It reminded me a lot of the challenge Dave gave us about accomplishing the things Jesus wants us to do."

"Jason, why did your Principal ask this guy to come to the school?"

"We were having some serious issues with our students. Sharon, our Principal, had about fifteen kids a month showing up in her office, and she felt she needed to do something. She heard about this guy from one of her colleagues and invited him. He had a profound impact on the kids, and since his talk, the number of kids showing up in Sharon's office has dropped to three a month."

"Jason, I would love to hear what that guy said; these are results you cannot argue with."

"Chris, he just spoke hope into the kids. He told them that they can make a difference, that they all have a role and a purpose, and that no one was put on the earth by accident. Lack of purpose is a big problem in our school, and we have a lot of kids who think they are just here by accident. They lack purpose and have no real-life goals. Wesley came from a broken home, and he was one of these kind of kids. His Dad left his Mom a year after Wesley was born, and he has not seen him since. Wesley took the speaker's message to heart. He started to serve his team and others, not for show, but because he wanted to. He seemed to see the broken and downcast and made a point of talking with them. As a result of all this, Wesley is now the captain of the football team. Chris, do you want to hear something remarkable that Wesley did last year at the Prom?"

"Sure, I would love to."

"We always have a Prom at the end of the school year. The school's general practice is that the Football Captain goes to the Prom with the head of the Cheerleaders. You know the story—the most beautiful girl in the school goes to the Prom with Captain of the Football Team."

"Jason, I know the story all too well. I was a geek in school with bad acne, and for most of the years, I did not even go to the Prom. Proms are a rather painful memory for me."

"Chris, that is the case for many of the kids in our school as well. The not so beautiful, unpopular, or less wealthy students find it a very uncomfortable experience. At any rate, Wesley has changed this whole experience for our students. At the dance, he noticed a grade nine girl that had a debilitating disease. She could not walk, and spent most of her time in a wheelchair. Wesley came to her and asked her to dance. She was shocked but agreed. Wesley picked her up in his arms, and he danced while carrying her in his arms. Her face lit up, and she was the belle of the ball. Her whole sense of self-worth changed in a moment. The whole school saw what Wesley did, and initially, they were shocked. Some were angry and started mocking him, yet others were moved with compassion and started to cry. It is amazing what one act of spontaneous kindness can do for a community. It brings out all kinds of emotions."

As I went home from the game, I felt convicted. How often had I seen a need and just not bothered to act? How often had I seen a person that was not that popular, perhaps a bit odd, and just ignored them? How often had I just not cared? Unfortunately, all too often. I prayed, "Father forgive me, for turning my eyes away from the hurting, and the downcast, and not wanting to get involved. Help me to see Jesus in people, give them eye contact, and show them I care. Please help me to do this." The words of Mother Teresa flooded into my mind. "I see Jesus in every human being. I say to myself, this one is hungry, Jesus; I must feed him. This one is sick, Jesus. This one has leprosy or gangrene; I must wash him and tend to him. I serve because I love Jesus."

Even at a football game, God can change our hearts.

---◆◆◆---

CHAPTER TEN

---◆◆◆---

Repentance

"Chris, I have good news," Dave said, "Cindy went for her checkup, and the number of tumours in her liver has gone down. The Doctor feels they could cut out the part of her liver with the remaining tumours, and she will be free from cancer. They told us they could cut away up to two-thirds of a liver, and it will grow back."

It had been about three months since Dave had told us about Cindy's condition. Linda and I met with Cindy weekly laying hands on her, imparting God's power, and rebuking the tumours in Jesus' name. We had read in the Bible that Jesus prayed for people more than once,[xiii] and the apostle Paul said one of the gifts of the Spirit was "the working of miracles."[xiv] We gathered from these examples that it wasn't a lack of faith to pray more than once.

We didn't know what we were doing. We just kept soaking Cindy in the anointing of God. Linda and I reasoned that you continually clean a wound when you have an infection and change the dressing and apply an antibiotic. We thought maybe working miracles was the same. It was not what we saw on TV. TV evangelists just seemed to lay hands on people and they were instantly healed. However, the proof is in the pudding. Cindy's tumours were leaving. I told Dave we would continue to pray for Linda, in the same way, every week, believing God to remove all of the tumours.

In this world, people want instant results. There is instant coffee, a one-minute breakfast, and fast food, yet God seems to be on a different timeline. He's not in a hurry. He is like a master violin maker who carefully designs and makes each part of the instrument fit together perfectly, carefully adjusting the pieces and applying just the right finish to bring out the best tones. It takes time.

God seemed to want to develop this practice in Linda and me and challenge us to press on to the high calling of healing the sick. However, it takes more time than we thought, more effort, and more persistence. We knew that if we consistently cleansed and freshly bandaged a wound, it would eventually heal. I believe miracles may often happen in the same way. Perhaps it gets faster the more we do it.

The marketplace was humming one Saturday. Joseph's stall was busy. It seemed he had a bumper crop and had more produce than ever. I said, "Joseph, this is amazing. Look at the size of your carrots. They are like zucchinis. What did you do? What fertilizer did you use?"

He said, "I did not do anything different than what I normally do. I use natural fertilizer each year, but this year each day, I got down on my knees and laid my hands on my ground, and I asked God to soak my land in His presence and to heal my land. I read in the Bible that 'If my people…will humble themselves and pray…[God] will hear from heaven…and heal their land.'xv I knew my land needed to be healed. The previous owner did not do proper crop rotation, and as a result, the soil was depleted, and it would take years to restore the earth. I started by repenting on behalf of the previous owner for not taking care of the land. Then I asked God to heal my land. Although, as I mentioned, I had also started to rehabilitate the soil, nothing I could have done accounts for this type of bumper crop. I can only think it was the result of my prayers."

I thought about what Joseph told me. I pondered if God can heal his physical land, perhaps He could improve our town's economy. We had once been a real thriving community. We had had four major manufacturers in our town; however, each company had closed their plants over time, and the buildings had been left vacant. The impact was felt immediately in our retail sector. Stores closed, and soon we did not have the money to repair our city's infrastructure, and we started to have potholes on our streets. Some people grumbled about the big internationals taking the jobs to other countries where labour was cheaper. But I knew there was more to the story.

We had had several significant strikes in our plants over the years. The Unions in our towns were mighty, and they did not work well with management. The first manufacturer to close could not agree with the Union and, after a nine-month strike, the company announced they would be closing the plant. The company did not leave the country. They just moved the factory 100 miles away into another county. Their bargaining agreement with the Union said that if they built another plant within 100 miles, it had to be Unionized, so they made the new plant over 100 miles away and continued to operate in our country. We had not lost the jobs to another country. We lost them to another county.

Our town started to get a reputation as an unreasonable Union town. Prospective companies interested in the vacant manufacturing plants decided not to locate in our city due to our reputation. Over the next few years, the other factories closed as well, leaving us with no significant employers. I thought about this and what Joseph had told me and wondered if we could heal our town. It had been over twenty years since the first factory closed, and our little village had shrunk in size. Perhaps we could reverse this.

The Cozy Corner restaurant was hopping on Saturday morning. All the men were talking like magpies. Each of them had a story to tell about how God had been talking to them and giving them ideas. Jason told us how he had presented his plan to the city Council to improve our town's economy. He also announced that he planned to run for a Councillor position in the next municipal election.

Paul talked about the button idea and how he could help others with their cars now without losing money. He said that his business had grown, and he had to hire a new mechanic. Joseph told about praying for his soil and how his carrots and produce had multiplied. This caught everybody's interest.

I said I thought about what Joseph had done and wondered if that might work for our economy. Maybe we could go out to the old factories and lay hands on them and bless them. Perhaps God would bless our town and heal our economy. The guys wanted to go out right away. Once men get stirred up, they want to act, not just talk.

I told the men Joseph had built his request before God on the Scripture, "If my people, who are called by my name, will humble themselves and pray and seek my face and turn from their wicked ways, then I will hear from heaven, and I will forgive their sin and will heal their land."[xvi] I wondered if we needed to humble ourselves and ask God to forgive us as a town for being so difficult with the factory owners.

Thomas spoke up immediately; he was pretty agitated. Thomas was the Union steward at one of the closed plants. He said, "Those sons of bitches threw us out on the street and didn't deal fairly with us. They wanted us to cut back some of our hard-earned benefits. We weren't going to let them do that. We had a membership to protect and families who depended on those benefits."

I said, "Thomas, I realize that there were wrong things done in several of those plant closures, and perhaps the companies were too demanding, but was it possible that we were too inflexible as well? Our town has a reputation for being a hardnosed Union town, and companies don't want to risk their shareholder's money in the cost it will take to retool our old factories. Could we have been a bit more flexible in our negotiations?"

Thomas sat quietly; I knew he knew the severity of the situation. I also knew Tom took his role as the Union steward seriously and had fought hard for his membership to secure those benefits. It would have been a tremendous personal loss if he gave back those hard-won concessions.

I continued, "Thomas, I know companies are cutting costs and benefits everywhere, not just here. I don't work for a Unionized company and don't have the benefit of having someone like you to go to our aid and fight for us, but it seems all companies are cutting benefits."

Lee spoke up, "At our company, we call it the 'Benefits Reduction Program.'" Lee was an investment counselor at a large bank. Several of the other guys nodded their heads, saying that every year their benefits had gone down.

I continued, "Let's humble ourselves before the Lord and ask His forgiveness for not being flexible enough. Perhaps we could ask His forgiveness for not being thankful for what we had and ask Him to heal our land. What do you think, Thomas?"

Tears started to well up in his eyes, and he said, "There's not a day goes by that I don't think about the impact of my decision to fight the management and not to give an inch. I wonder if I had just given a bit, would we still have the factories?"

Thomas hung his head and prayed, "God, I'm sorry for failing my members. I should have been more flexible. Forgive me for my pride, my arrogance, and the impact on my town. Forgive us for not listening to the management when they told us about the financial troubles. I also forgive them for not dealing with their excesses and wastes. Please forgive us and heal our community. Please bring factories back to our town, so our kids don't have to leave to find work."

As I looked around the table, there was not a dry eye in the house. Thomas's humility and brokenness had touched all of us. All knelt in agreement.

I know God heard that prayer.

CHAPTER ELEVEN

Heal Our Land

After breakfast, we piled into our cars and drove out to the old factories, and as a group, we laid hands on the buildings and asked God to heal our land. We called the jobs back. We rebuked any lying and deceiving spirits that had come against our community and forbid them to speak lies about us. We spoke prosperity over potential employers and blessed our town.

Pastor Dave reminded us of a Scripture that told us that we have the authority to bind and loose.[xvii] He said, "Binding and loosing was an old Hebrew practice that a Rabbi did to interpret the law. It was a type of poetic saying. It meant to forbid or permit. A Rabbi would interpret the law and say whether the Law forbids something or permits it. The Lord has given us the same authority to bind and loosen things. We have the authority to forbid or permit things in the spiritual realm."

Dave went on to explain, "The apostle tells us that we wrestle not against flesh and blood, but against principalities and powers in high places.[xviii] There are evil power structures set up on the earth. They draw their rights to be present based on the sins of man. The more a group thinks the same way, and the more those thought patterns are sinful, the stronger the demonic stronghold becomes. For instance, during the Second World War in Germany, people believed that the Jews were not people and should not live. This was an example of groupthink, and the demonic exploited this, and six million Jews died. It also shows up when people embrace prejudice and racial superiority thoughts. Christians are not immune to this kind of blind groupthink. In the southern States two centuries ago, 4000 blacks were lynched by people who went to church every Sunday, because they believed that blacks were less than human. We must always examine what we believe and be transformed by the renewing of our minds, and not let groupthink rule in our lives."

I had never heard Pastor Dave talk like this; this was not your standard Sunday morning sermon; everyone was riveted to his words. He went on to say, "We can defeat these structures by doing what we did in the café. We repent for the sins of those who went before us and for ourselves, and then go on the offensive and command the demonic spirits to leave based on the fact that they have no right to stay.

"This type of prayer is called intercession. It is a special type of prayer. It is the type of prayer Moses did when he stood between God and the children of Israel. God says, 'I look for someone to stand in the gap.'[xix] That is a poetic way of saying 'I'm looking for someone who would repent on behalf of a people group,' an appeal to God for forgiveness and healing. Prayer is much more than a series of requests between man and God. It's a joint venture between God and man to bring His kingdom to this earth." Dave's words struck us all, and we realized that we all had allowed groupthink to form in our hearts and given the demonic some rights over our town. We knew repentance was necessary to break this situation, and quietly men hung their heads and asked God for His forgiveness. Many men's eyes welled up with tears; some began to sob gently.

The last plant we stopped at was Clifford Glass. Thomas had been the Union steward for Clifford Glass. A chain-link fence surrounded the plant, and the gate was locked. We could not get to the building, so we stood in a circle in front of the entrance. To our surprise, Caleb stepped forward and took out his keys, and unlocked the gate.

Caleb, a heavy-set man in his sixties, had been the Clifford plant manager before it closed. He turned to Thomas and said, "Thomas, it was not your fault alone that this plant closed. I, too, am to blame. Your prayer deeply moved me at the Diner, and the Lord convicted me. Blaming the Union for the plant closure was easy. The truth is I could have taken a lot more leadership with my company and management team. We were paid on bonuses. I could have cut out all bonuses until the plant was profitable. I could have implemented a profit-sharing plan and helped our workers participate in the profits when things went well. I could have shown a lot more flexibility, as well. I could have drastically simplified the management layers. I could have dealt more effectively with quality problems. I could have invested in a disciplined approach to eliminating defects from the manufacturing processes, such as Six Sigma training for all my staff, and I could have introduced a product quality bonus program for your Union friends. I could have done all that, but I didn't. I should have worked with you to resolve our issues, but I let my pride rule, and I stuck to my old-school positional bargaining posture and didn't give creativity any room.

"Please forgive me, Thomas? I ask all of you as representatives of the town to forgive me. I also need to humble myself before the Lord before we pray for this plant. Lord, forgive me. I was not a good leader. I was selfish, greedy, inflexible, and wanted to blame the Union for our problems. Forgive me, Father, for I have sinned. Please break off this plant the reputation of being a difficult place to do business. Please loosen favour over this plant, and please break off of our town the impact of what I have sown and anything we are reaping as a result of my sins."

Thomas went up to Caleb, put his arm around his shoulder, and together they embraced, wept, and forgave each other. All we could do was look on in shock. Two sworn enemies forgave each other on the very ground where they had so fiercely fought.

God was, indeed, coming to our town.

GREENVILLE
[CHRISTIAN CHURCH]
SUNDAY 10:00

JESUS MESSIAH
PRINCE OF PEACE
KING OF LOVE

CHAPTER TWELVE

Battlefield of the Mind

Dave declared, "The kingdom of God is at hand," from his pulpit the following Sunday morning. "Jesus talked about the kingdom of God more than He talked about anything else. He only spoke about the Church two times, but He talked about the kingdom of God eighty times. In the book of Matthew, the kingdom of God is called 'the kingdom of Heaven.' It would have been offensive to the people to say the kingdom of God. When Jesus talked about the kingdom of God, He used different phrases. He uses three specific sayings, and each one has a different meaning. Let's look at them together. Jesus said, "The kingdom of God is at hand.[xx] The kingdom of God is within you.[xxi] The kingdom of God has come upon you."[xxii] Each phrase meant something different."

Something had happened to Dave. He always preached messages from the Bible and related it to something we were facing, but there was a change. His preaching had much more depth. He no longer just told us stories which he supported with Scripture. He had started to open the Scriptures and explain them in detail. I felt like I was receiving a flow of revelation when he spoke and was being fed good food.

For some reason, I felt like I had been living on junk food, and now I was being fed a substantial balanced meal.

Dave told me that he was concerned with what he called Biblical illiteracy. He said, "I have noticed over the last few years that the overall level of Bible knowledge is going down. Few people bring Bibles to church anymore, and I feel that I need to do something about this. It has been a primary prayer focus in my life." From this morning's sermon, it was clear Dave had decided to do something about it.

"Let's look at each of these statements Jesus said, in detail," Dave declared. "'The kingdom of God is at hand.' We choose every day whether we will be in the kingdom of God and allow His kingdom principles and rules to reign or not. A kingdom is a place where a King rules. It is where his values, standards, and laws are followed. Each day we face choices. For example, when you are driving, and someone cuts you off, you can decide to bless the person or present them with the all too familiar one-finger salute. When we bless, we are letting the kingdom of God rule. When we blast the driver, we are not. Every day we are faced with choices like this."

This statement convicted me because all too often, I had given the one-finger salute when I drove. I remember reading about a man who imagined that he had a big red button on his dashboard that he would mash down when someone would cut him off, and he envisioned a rocket would launch from his car and blow up the other driver. I often wanted that red button.

Dave continued, "Each day, we are presented with situations that are beautiful to look at and things that are not. We choose to step into the kingdom of God based on what we think about and what we watch. A few years ago, a person wrote a book called *Battlefield of the Mind*.[xxiii] I believe our actions are always the result of what we think about or feel. The Bible gives us counsel about how we should think. It says, 'Whatsoever things are pure, lovely, of good report, think on these things.'[xxiv] As we choose to think about these things, we decide to step into the kingdom of God."

Dave hit home again. I knew that there were many movies and books that I had watched and read that were not righteous. I did not look at porn, but I sure loved a violent film. I started to think that perhaps this was not the best thing I could watch. I felt challenged to reexamine what I read and watched. I noticed several other people in the church were feeling uncomfortable. It was like God was putting his finger on many of our pet sins and saying, "It is time to change."

I felt a memory come back to me about an old manager named Doug. I hated this guy. I had had good managers over most of my career that respected my skills and contributions and asked for my advice. Doug was not like that. He had been hired from another company to manage our group. He did not have the same approach to management that other managers in our company had. We had embraced a servant leadership model, and Doug had an autocratic management style. Our managers spent time talking with you and were quite amiable. Doug was not like this. He was all business and did not care about your family or personal interests.

Doug only wanted to know how many products you had sold this week. He was relentless, never wanting to listen to my opinions. I consistently felt worthless when I was around him. He made everyone feel that way, not just me.

Week after week, after I met with him, I would have imaginary conversations with him where I would tell him off. Imaginary conversations were a problem I had always had. I would often have imaginary conversations with people after some conflict. When I talked with them, I would be gracious, but I would take a piece off them in my mind. I would say things like, "You enjoy your power because you are a small man who likes to beat up on us that have no authority. You are a real prick."

My thoughts were not very sanctified. I knew this was wrong, and I would often forgive Doug and repent of my judgments of him, but I still hated him. Eventually, I got so fed up, I applied for another job and transferred out of Doug's department. As Dave spoke, I thought about all this, and I knew that I needed God's help to get free from these conversations. Later I took out my journal and asked the Lord, "Why did you give me a manager like Doug?" A flow of thoughts came to mind. I felt He said:

"Chris,

"You had become very comfortable in your job. You did not have to work very hard, and it was not that difficult. You were coasting. I did not want you to coast. I wanted you to learn about new technologies. I wanted you to be current and relevant. I needed you to change your job, but you would never do that, so I sent Doug to motivate you to change. I discipline my children. 'No discipline seems pleasant at the time but painful. Later on, however, it produces a harvest of righteousness and peace for those trained by it.'[xxv] Doug was merely an instrument of my discipline.

"Love, Dad"

The flow of thoughts shook me up. I never thought that Doug was God's instrument of discipline. I just thought of him as a pain in the ass who cared about his career. The Bible says, "The steps of a good man are ordered by the Lord: and he delighteth in his way."[xxvi] I had never even thought that hardship or tough bosses could be God's will, but in this case, it was.

I felt a transformation start to happen in my heart. I realized for the first time that Doug was part of God's will for my life. I thanked God that He motivated me to change. My new job was far better than my old job, and I was enjoying it. It was tough, and I had to learn a lot of new technology, but it was all right.

A quote from W. Edwards Deming came to my mind. He said, "It is not necessary to change. Survival is not mandatory." My Heavenly Father wanted me to survive, so He arranged for me to be changed.

CHAPTER THIRTEEN

Loss

A s usual, the Cozy Corners restaurant was alive with activity and laughter; every member of the men's group seemed to want to talk. I was amazed. The place was active, guys were showing up early, and unlike previous meetings, cars and trucks were not the objects of their conversation. Each person was talking about what God was showing them. Mike, the mechanic at the garage, came in last. He looked like a disaster. His hair was unkempt, unshaven, and his eyes were red. Mike was not like this. He always prided himself on looking good. His jet-black hair that was now going salt and pepper, was always trimmed and neat. Jim said, "Mike, what happened to you?"

Mike looked up and said, "Sandra died." The place went deadly quiet, and Mike collapsed in tears and started to wail.

Mike's wife, Sandra, was well known as being the best cook in the church. Her Italian heritage heavily influenced her culinary expertise, and we always looked forward to her contributions to potluck dinners. "What happened, Mike?" Jim asked.

"Last night after supper, Sandra said, 'I don't feel well. I think I will go upstairs and lie down.' I told her, 'No problem. I will clean up the dishes and the kitchen; go and have a rest.' Those were the last words I spoke to her. I watched a couple of TV shows and decided to go up to bed. I noticed that Sandra was lying in bed. She looked asleep. I did not want to disturb her, but I knew Sandra would not want to go to bed that way. I spoke to her and gave her a little touch, and she didn't respond. I noticed that something was wrong. Then I noticed she wasn't breathing. I put my arms around her, and she just laid there in my arms motionless, limp like a bunny. I knew she was gone. I didn't know what to do. Tears filled my eyes, and I started to howl, 'Why God? Why did you take her?' I called 911, and the paramedics were there in minutes, but they could do nothing. Sandra had slipped away hours before."

Paul asked, "What happened?" Mike replied, "The Doctor at the hospital said she had a heart attack." "Heart attack! Sandra is only fifty-nine years old, and she was not overweight. How can that be?" Paul exclaimed." "The Doctor told me that although she was not fat on the outside, she was fat on the inside. They said when plaque builds up, it narrows the coronary arteries and can cause a heart attack. Rich foods probably caused it. I couldn't believe his words; I had always loved her cooking, but it killed her. I thought if I had only gone up to the room after cleaning up the kitchen, perhaps, I would have seen she was in trouble and got help earlier."

The room was silent. The entire group was in shock; all we could hear was Mike sobbing. Then Cliff Wallace stepped forward and put his arms around Mike and started to cry. Cliff had lost his wife about a year ago to pancreatic cancer. As these two men embraced, I saw other men come around them both. All the men were wiping tears from their eyes. Some were quietly praying. Others were just quiet. As I stood there, the Scripture "Jesus wept"[xxvii] came to my mind. When Jesus' friend Lazarus died, and Jesus went to comfort his sisters, His first response was to weep with Mary and Martha. When someone dies, tears seem to be the best thing we can say.

No one felt like eating, and after a while, Paul and Cliff left with Mike to help him arrange the funeral. I noticed that all the rest of the guys took out their cell phones and called their wives to tell them the news and say to them that they loved them.

At times of loss, we remember to treasure those closest to us.

CHAPTER FOURTEEN

Murderball

Sunday morning, we were back in church, and Dave had decided to continue his series on the Kingdom of God. Dave started by declaring, "The kingdom of God is within you. In everyone's heart, there are compartments or rooms where the Lord stands at the door and knocks. We have the choice to let Him in or not. If we let Him into those rooms, His kingdom comes in. I believe this is what it means when He says, 'The kingdom of God is within you.' All of us have had dramatic events that hold pain for us that we would rather forget. Many have experienced abuse and suffered from memories that rob them of life, and they have locked those doors. Others have committed sins that they are ashamed of and have locked those doors in fear that others may find out and expose them.

"The Lord stands at the door of all these locked rooms and knocks. He asks to come in and bring His kingdom. In His kingdom, there is no pain, no shame, and no fear. There is a peace that passes all understanding. We have to decide to let Him in. As we do, the kingdom of God is within us."

I noticed that many people started to hang their heads and wipe their eyes. One of Linda's friends began to cry, and Linda went to her and consoled her. I felt a draw on my heart like I wanted to get on my knees and repent. I was all of a sudden aware of sins I had forgotten, both sins I had committed and sins others had done to me. I could not shake the feeling. I had read about revivals under Charles Finney, how churches were convicted of their sins and mistakes and wanted to get right with God. I wondered if that was happening to us. It was indeed something I had never experienced in church before.

As I sat there, another memory came to me.

A couple of months ago, I was participating in a company golf game. I am not a very good golfer, but I enjoy the camaraderie of playing with a team. There was a golf pro there from the PGA who was famous. Everyone was getting their picture taken with him, so I lined up to get my photo taken as well.

For reasons I did not understand, instead of the Golf Pro just having his picture taken with the next person in line, he seemed to choose people at random. He continually refused to pick me. It seemed odd at first, but as time wore on, he steadily declined to pick me. I was starting to get mad. I wanted to give him the finger and tell him off. He reminded me of so many jocks I had known over my life. He was six foot four, perfect hair, perfect teeth, tanned, all muscle, and a total jerk.

I was outraged. Eventually, the Pro did pick me when there was nobody else left.

I remember stewing about this guy for days. I would think about him during the day. I wrote a letter of complaint to the company about his behaviour, but I didn't feel any better.

I asked the Lord, "Why do I feel this way? Why does this guy's behaviour bug me so much?" A flow of thoughts came to my mind again. I thought He said:

"Son,

"Forgive the PGA Pro. A deep sense of rejection causes your feelings. You remember in your heart not being picked at school for sports because you were small. This happened often, and as a result, when you were not chosen, it felt like rejection. Your heart ties into the pain of the past and the unforgiveness and judgments of the past.

"Son,

"Forgive those who did not pick you when you were young. Forgive them for not choosing you and preferring bigger kids. Repent of your judgments that these leaders were favourite driven, unjust, brutal, malicious, and unkind to you personally.

"Son, the anger will leave you.

"Love, Dad"

The pain of my childhood came flooding back to me. I was small when I entered high school. Only 4' 9." There were guys in my class a foot taller. Their favourite game was a type of dodge ball called murderball. I was the last to get picked and the first to get hammered by a ball. It got so bad that, as soon as gym was an elective, I stopped taking gym. I profoundly despised the jocks.

These were doors in my heart that I had locked. Today the Lord was standing at that door and was knocking. He wanted to heal the little boy trapped in the pain of the past.

I chose to answer His knock, forgave those jocks, and I was set free.

CHAPTER FIFTEEN

Revival

"Lastly," Dave said, "'The kingdom of God comes upon us.' This phrase has to do with the kingdom of God manifesting itself in power. When miracles are released, the kingdom of God comes upon us. When Jesus imparted healing to a person, the kingdom of God was manifested in the person's body. In the kingdom of God, there is no sickness and no death. When we pray for the sick and step into the authority we have been given, we too impart healing, and the kingdom of God comes upon that person, and God rules over the illness and healing starts happening.

"Sometimes, it is immediate, like when Jesus told the man with the withered hand to stretch out his arm.[xxviii] As the man stretched out his hand, flesh immediately came back onto the man's hand. Instant healing also happened with a woman who was subject to bleeding for twelve years. When she touched the hem of Jesus' garment, her bleeding instantly stopped.[xxix] Then there were other cases where time was involved. For example, when Jesus prayed for the ten lepers. It says that as they went, they were healed.[xxx] Sometime later, they recognized they were healed. Unfortunately, only one returned to thank Jesus."

"Once Jesus healed a blind man by spitting into his eyes. When Jesus asked, 'Do you see anything?' He said, 'I see men as trees walking.' Jesus prayed for him again, and then he could see clearly. Jesus heals many different ways—sometimes immediately, sometimes over time, and sometimes due to the persistence of the one who is praying. In all these cases, the healing is a demonstration of the kingdom of God."

Cindy stood up and began to speak. Dave and Cindy would often preach like a tag team. Cindy was an excellent preacher, and we looked forward to hearing what she had to say. "Six months ago, I was diagnosed with bowel cancer." There was a wave of horror that went over the church as Cindy spoke. "I had cancer removed, but my doctor gave me more bad news when she said that cancer had metastasized and was spreading to other organs. She told me that she saw tumours in my liver. I had already developed stage IV cancer and was not expected to live long.

"I did not want to tell anyone. Both my parents died of cancer, and I remembered how people would look at them with pity. I did not want to experience this. When you cry out to God for healing and your faith is almost gone, the last thing you need is some well-meaning soul pitying you and saying some type of pithy Christian saying. You also don't want to hear someone say, 'What did you do? What did you eat? Do have you have any idea how this could come upon you?' It implies that somehow you brought this upon yourself. You just need someone to speak faith into your heart so you can continue to believe for another day.

"About three months ago, Dave mentioned that I was sick to a close friend, and he came over with his wife and asked if they could practice healing the sick. He said the seventy-two disciples were sent out to heal the sick. Those words challenged me. They laid hands on me, and instead of saying beautiful prayers, they commanded the tumours in my liver to shrink and leave in Jesus' name. They loosened healing into my body, and I felt the power of God come over me, and there was a tangible sense of heat on my back. Every week for the last three months, this couple has repeated this activity.

"I went to my doctor this week, and she said, 'Cindy, there has been a change. There are fewer tumours in your liver. I think we can operate and remove the part of your liver that has the remaining tumours.' I am preparing to have this surgery as we speak. I also plan to continue with my chemo, but it is undeniable I have experienced a miracle. Cancer has stopped spreading in my liver, and the tumours are going away."

The church erupted with hollering and whistling. People began standing, raising their hands and shouting, praising God. We were not a demonstrative church, so this was entirely unexpected. Cindy then said, "If there is anyone here who is sick, I encourage you to come to the front, and we will anoint you with oil, lay hands on you, and impart healing." Almost the entire church came forward.

Men and women came to the front. Some were weeping and asking God for forgiveness, some were kneeling and quietly crying, and others started laughing as a spirit of joy came over them. Many still had tears in their eyes, but a feeling of joy seemed to overwhelm them. Dave and Linda started praying for people, and the people seemed to lose all their strength and fell to the ground. Fortunately, others around them caught them, so they did not get hurt.

The ministry time went on for an hour, and the people covered the floor, seemingly unable or not wanting to get up. It was like they were just resting in God. I had heard about being slain in the Spirit, and I had seen TV evangelists pray for people, and they had fallen, but this was the first time I had seen it for myself. I knew this was real. You could not have paid them to fall. I was looking at a revival, the kind I had read about in books.

The kingdom of God had come to Greenville Community Church that day. I knew we would never be the same.

CHAPTER SIXTEEN

Stewardship

"I need extra snack food this weekend, Calvin. My grandchildren and family are coming over for a pool party," I exclaimed.

"Happy to meet your every need," Calvin replied.

Calvin and his wife had come to Greenville about twelve years ago from Korea and managed our local convenience store ever since. Calvin had grown the business, and he now sells pizza, has a small bakery, a DVD rental business, a liquor store, and a florist all in one shop. Calvin has done very well. Every morning and night I drop-in, and he is there. I wondered if he ever slept.

"Calvin, I notice you're always here. When do you sleep?"

Calvin replied, "I get about four to six hours every night. I only work about eighty hours a week."

"Eighty hours a week! Calvin, that's insane."

"Chris, you have to do this if you want to survive in my kind of business. We grow up learning to work long hours in Korea. We all work 5½ days a week there, and they are long days."

As I left the store, I thought, "Wow, are we soft. We work 37.5 hours a week and complain about that." It made me feel, though, how hard it must be for Calvin's family. When did they ever take a holiday? Calvin and Joyce are very faithful to attend our church. They are firm believers, and their entire family works in the store. They always seem to be happy. Calvin would give you the shirt off his back, and I don't know anyone who works as hard as he does. Occasionally, he has come to the men's breakfast, but he cannot often attend due to his business demands.

I thought about this, and I wondered how we could help him. He has all the needs of any other family. He has to look after his house, cut his grass, paint the fence, etc. I have been to his home, and I have noticed that many chores were not getting done. I wondered if perhaps the men's group might be able to get involved and help him somehow. I reached out to Dave and discussed the situation. He said he would bring it up at our next meeting.

"I will have three eggs over easy, home fries, bacon and sausage, and a pail of coffee." Jim was back in full form; however, instead of the Farmers' breakfast, he had made a slight adjustment by cutting out the pancakes. "I have to watch my figure," Jim said. "My doctor said I have to lose some weight, so I thought I would start by cutting out the pancakes."

Dave spoke up and said, "Perhaps some fruit might help you lose some weight. I had to go on a strict diet of oatmeal and fruit a few years ago, and it helped me lose weight and get my cholesterol down."

"I'm not sure I can change that fast, Dave," said Jim, "but at least I'm starting with something."

As usual, the topic of cars came up. Joseph told the group about his 1948 truck, and everyone was captivated by Paul's 1965 Shelby Mustang. Thomas spoke up and said he had just acquired a 1959 Buick LeSabre. It had only 25,000 miles on it and still had the original paint. Mike immediately spoke up and said, "Sweet. That car is a monster, but parts are tough to get for it."

Thomas replied, "It was sitting in a lady's garage since it was new, and she only drove a few miles a year. It seems to have an oil leak around the transmission."

"That is the rear seal. That's a tough part to find, but I'll start making some inquires for you on Monday," declared Mike. Mike loved to get these old cars running again, but there was more to this sudden urge to help Thomas. The whole group started going the extra mile for each other, even Mike.

Soon everyone was talking about the things they were doing to accomplish what they felt Jesus was doing. Jason succeeded in getting elected to our Council, and he had found several companies expressing interest in moving to our town. I felt like things were improving, and there was excitement in the air.

Dave spoke up, "I am so amazed at the things you all are doing. I am impressed by your creativity. You are all good stewards." Dave continued, "Stewardship is not a word we use much today. Jesus once told a parable about three servants that a man left in charge of his property when he went on a trip. To one servant he gave five talents, to another two talents, and another one talent." Dave explained, "A talent was a commercial weight used in ancient times. In this case, he gave them talents of silver or gold. When the owner returned from his trip, he called his servants and asked them to account for what they had done with the money he had given them. Jesus used this story to explain the kingdom of God. He said that there would be a time when we will have to give account to the Lord regarding how we have invested the gifts He has given us. There are three categories of things He gives us: finances, skills, and time."

Don, the Cozy Corner restaurant owner, spoke up and said, "Dave, are you saying we have to prove that we are worthy of going to Heaven? We are saved by grace."

Dave replied, "Don, you are right. Grace, not works save us. We are granted access to Heaven because of the sacrifice of Jesus. Our Heavenly Father loves us and accepts us just as we are. This parable is not about a judgment regarding our access to Heaven. It has more to do with our responsibilities when we get there. The Lord is looking for good stewards, and Jesus is talking about that in this parable." Don still seemed to feel uncomfortable with that answer.

Lee (an Investment broker) noticed this and suggested, "Don, if I invest your money, you expect me to ensure a good return. You would not be pleased with me if I just put your money in an account that did not give you a return."

"That's for sure," Don replied.

Lee continued, "It is a lot of work to find good investment vehicles that match your risk profile, Don. I take my job very seriously, and it takes time and talent, and a little luck to ensure I invest your money wisely. If I don't do this well, I won't be allowed to stay in investment banking."

Don seemed to be at peace with that answer. Dave commented, "I believe we need to examine ourselves and judge ourselves regarding our use of our gifts, and if we are not using them well, we need to make some changes. I want you to write down what you are good at and what you like to do in a notebook. We'll call these our 'signature strengths.'" Dave gave each of us a small notebook and a pen. I started writing out what my signature strengths were. It was a bit hard at first, and then I thought, "I like to write, and I enjoy public speaking. I'm a good musician, and I love to lead worship. I listen well and seem to be able to give good advice." Pretty soon, the page was full.

Dave asked everyone to read out a couple of signature strengths that we had written down. Joseph said, "I'm good at growing crops and playing guitar." Paul said, "I am a good mechanic and like to draw and photograph things." Soon everyone had spoken. It was remarkable the strengths they came up with—teaching, painting houses, gardening, planning events, leading groups, designing buildings, fishing, and the list went on and on.

Dave said, "Great! Let's look at the next area. How do you spend your time? How many hours a day do you work, invest in your skills, entertain yourself, invest in your home, and invest in others?" He had us write this down, and we all realized we were spending too much time in front of the television, and that we could be using that time much more wisely.

Lastly, he said, "How do you spend your finances? Are you planning to give and planning to save?" Dave differed from many other preachers when it came to finances. He was always telling us to save for the future. He said, "The Bible tells us that a man who does not provide for his immediate family is worse than the heathen."[xxxi] He said, "The Greek word for 'provide' used here, is a future-oriented verb meaning 'to save for the future.' Most preachers, I knew always talked about giving but not about saving."

Dave said, "There are many worthy causes that we need to consider when investing our money. We need to see giving as investing. A good steward expects a good return even when it comes to giving. When you give to a charity, investigate how much is spent on charity versus administration and marketing. Review churches as well. It's a stewardship question. We need to invest in charities that use the money wisely.

"There is no end to demands for your money. We need to invest wisely. We need to fund our church and help individuals, particularly the widows and the orphans. Tax receipts should never be the motivation for deciding to whom we give. We need to listen to the Lord and use our minds to examine the cause and invest wisely. Write down how much you save and give, and ask yourself if you are spending your money wisely."

Jim piped up and said, "Dave, doesn't the Bible say that when we give money away, our right hand should not know what our left hand is doing?" Dave replied, "That's right, Jim, so please don't share this paper with anyone. All acts of philanthropy must always be done in secret."

Dave continued to speak, "Stewardship requires us to take our responsibility seriously, and it requires action. We are accountable for what we do with our gifts. A member of our men's ministry brought to my attention a situation in our church that I thought might help us be better stewards of our time, skills, and finances. He told me about a man who lives in our community who works eighty hours a week and cannot take care of his home, and really could use some practical help around the house.

I know of many single mothers and elderly folks that are in the same state. Many of them cannot afford much but are willing to pay for some help. But they cannot find anyone who will help them, and those who have helped them are ripping them off. I spoke to one older woman who was having trouble with her electrical outlet. It was sparking intermittently. She called an electrician, and he came and replaced the plug and charged her $400. It was robbery, but she had no choice. She didn't know what else to do."

I could see that Dave was getting excited about all this. His face seemed to shine, and he was becoming very animated. He continued, "I spoke with another member of our church who works with the federal revenue agency as a volunteer tax advisor. He helps people whose spouses have died and need help to do their taxes. It's straightforward for him. He has a strong financial background and is retired, and it is a great gift to those people he's helping. I propose we create a Greenville Community Church job jar. We can likely use the church website to facilitate this, and connect people who have jobs needing to be done with people who have the skills that want to do it. What do you think?"

The group loved the idea. Richard Brown offered, "I would be happy to coordinate this." Dave replied, "Thanks Richard. Now I encourage all of us to keep our eyes open for opportunities where help is needed and let Richard know, and also start looking for opportunities to start volunteering. Not everyone is going to ask for help, but we can all offer to help."

It was a great meeting. We all started thinking about how we could be much better stewards of our talents, time, and finances. Dave closed the session by saying, "How many of you have ever wished you could play the piano, or could go and see the Rocky Mountains? The truth is you can do this if you plan to do it. We all have the same amount of time in a day. We just need to decide how we will use it."

Dave continued, "The last category I want you to write in your book is called your 'bucket list.' I want you to write down all the things you want to do, learn, and want to see. Once you have made this initial list, I encourage you to continue adding to it every time you think of something you want to see or do. I do this. I add places I want to see to my list all the time, and every year Cindy and I plan a trip to go and see some of them."

All of the men started to talk like magpies. Each one spoke about their dreams, hopes, and desires. It was interesting to hear all the ideas. Some wanted to travel. Others wanted to own a cottage. Some wanted to go on a mission trip. The list was endless. Caleb told me a story last week that he had always wanted to learn to play the violin, so when he was forty-eight years old, he bought an old violin and took some lessons. Although he didn't play very well, he kept working on it. Caleb is now sixty-three and loves to play his violin.

Caleb told me about another man in his business who was about fifty-two years old and wanted to learn French. Some people told him he was too old to learn a new language because his brain wouldn't adjust. He surprised them all and became fluent in French. Caleb said, "Never give up on your dreams. Never let anyone tell you you're too old to do something."

The group started to write, and as they wrote, they became happier and happier. It was like their youth's dreams began to flow back into their minds, and they started to dream again.

Dave concluded our meeting by saying, "The Psalmist says, 'Delight in the Lord and He will give you the desires of your heart.' The Lord wants to give you the things you have written on your bucket list. Just delight in Him, and He will do it."

I wrote my list, and the first thing I wrote was that I wanted to learn to ride a motorcycle.

CHAPTER SEVENTEEN

Kids

"Dad, why would God require Abraham to kill Isaac? You have taught me that God is love, but this is not loving. Would you kill me if God told you to?" Mark, my son, asked some of the most challenging and profound questions. He was not a boy that was satisfied with simple answers. He wanted the truth. I wondered, "How do I answer this question?" When faced with challenging problems at work or home, I have a standard reply. I call out to the Lord and ask for help. I asked the Lord how I should answer this. I felt a still small voice in my mind begin to speak to me. I thought He said:

"Son,

"Abraham believed in his heart that if I asked him to kill his son, I would raise him again immediately. If you read the account, you'll understand that Abraham said to Isaac that they were going up to the mountains to sacrifice, and they would return. He knew that I would not allow Isaac to die. I have never asked anyone to do this again, and I never will. I sent my Son Jesus to take the place of the sacrifice, but He was not left in the grave. He was raised to life. Son, Mark is afraid you love Me more than him. Tell him you do love Me more than anyone, but you love your family to the point of giving up your life for them."

"Love, Dad"

I thanked the Lord and felt I would have something to tell Mark if this question came up again. Linda and I had raised our family in the nurture and admonition of the Lord. Unfortunately, it was at a time when religion was harsher. It was at a time when many Scriptures were bent to support pet doctrines and outright errors. We also did not have a good revelation of our Heavenly Father's heart for us. We did not understand that nurture and admonition involved intimacy and kindness.

The impact, unfortunately, on our kids was that they were not all sold on Christianity. I've often had regrets regarding how much time we spent in church activities, and I realize now I should have spent more time doing personal fathering with my children. The challenge I faced was how to rectify these mistakes of the past. I had a talk with Pastor Dave about it. Dave has four children; two are serving the Lord, two are not. I asked Dave, "What do I do regarding my children?"

"Chris, first be easier on yourself," encouraged Dave. "The children today will be better parents than we were because they know many things we did not know. However, we were better parents than our parents were, and they were better parents than their parents were. Parents today are taught to reason more with their children, to invest in them. They are not as selfish as our generation. They also know the impact of corporal punishment. Our parents and we did not know this.

"Chris, we were both raised in a legalistic faith, where God was a big cop in the sky who had a big stick that would whack us if we did anything wrong. We were told, "You spare the rod, you spoil the child,"[xxxii] so we spanked our children, and we were harsh in the way we disciplined them. We did not understand that this verse had to do with our responsibility to correct our children, not corporal punishment. We made a lot of mistakes. However, God's able to fix our errors. He's ready to restore and rebuild relationships.

"I know of one family whose home was very violent, and eventually, the woman divorced her husband. Amazingly, after two years, the man became a believer and changed. The woman's love for him returned, and they remarried. God can heal relationships and restore the years the locust has eaten.[xxxiii]

"I've also seen Pastors' boys who turned away from God and lived very ungodly lives, but God wooed them back. God can heal our family relationships and our kids' hearts from our mistakes. I believe the key is to practice humility, admit your mistakes, ask forgiveness, and continue to love and be there for them. Woo them as our Heavenly Father woos us."

"Dave, how do I help them understand the stories in the Bible like when God asked Abraham to kill Isaac, or Lot sleeping with his daughters? How about when God told Israel to kill all the people in the Promised Land? How do I answer these questions when they ask, 'Where is your loving God in these situations?'"

"Chris, let's look at each story. Abraham knew God was a loving God and would not allow Isaac to die. He knew that if God asked for this, He would raise him. Lot's daughters had become influenced by the people in their community and manipulated Lot. Now, why would Lot allow this to happen? Perhaps he thought humanity was wiped out, and he would have to start humanity over; maybe he was not as righteous as we think. I only know the Bible does not cover up the sins of its heroes. It would have been easy for the writer to leave out that part. Perhaps it's a warning that just because you've done some great thing for God, do not think you can't fail. Moses failed, as well. He had an anger problem all his life. When God told him to speak to the rock, he struck it with his rod, probably in anger, and as a result, Moses did not enter the Promised Land."

"Dave, that helps. Thanks. I know that my kids love me. I know they are thankful for the life we provided for them, and I just wish I could help them in the area of their faith. The internet seems to be a never-ending source of misinformation. One day my son sent me a site of a guy that challenged our faith, and as a result of his dissertation, my son believes the Bible is false. I started to look up each Scripture, and the guy had misquoted and twisted each verse. I looked on the site for some way to get hold of this guy, and there was no way to contact him. It was very frustrating."

"Chris, what were you like when you were a teenager?"

"Oh, I was a very outspoken critic of my parents' church. It was a liberal church that did not believe in any of the gifts of the Spirit. I once asked my Pastor why God did not do miracles anymore. He said that miracles passed away with apostles. I could not believe that. I talked with a teacher at my school about this, and he said that was not true, and as a result of this teacher's influence, I became deeply involved with what people now call the New Age movement for eight years."

"How did you get out of that?" Dave asked.

Chris declared, "I had a horrible experience at one of the meetings. I became terrified. I realized that I was alone and that all my spiritual knowledge did not bring me peace or comfort. My mother-in-law had been attending Charismatic meetings, and she invited my then-girlfriend (Linda) and I to attend. I did not want to go, but Linda did, so I went. The meeting was not like anything I had ever seen. Men were singing with all their might, and they were raising their hands in worship. I also felt something that I had never experienced. I felt the presence of God.

"I went forward to the front with Linda, and we knelt and cried. Although we did not pray a sinner's prayer, I felt this was what Christ's Church was supposed to be. I was deeply impacted. I was happy after that. About three months later, I went to a Full Gospel Business Men's breakfast. Men laid their hands on Linda and I, and the Holy Spirit flowed over us. I was radically changed, and I wanted to tell everyone that they needed to be filled with the Holy Spirit."

Dave said, "Chris, you were drawn by the Lord, and He worked out all the details. I am confident your parents were concerned about you and prayed for you. God answered that prayer. You would have likely not listened to them if they had tried to show you the error of your ways. God works all things together for the good of those who have been called according to His purpose.[xxxiv] You need to let go of your kids now and let God draw them. Trust Him; He wants them to know Him. Do you pray for them?"

"Dave, I have to admit I have not been faithful to do this, but that'll change as a result of our discussion today."

"Chris, pray that your kids would know their destiny and become the people God made them to be. Take authority over the lies that come against them, and pray that they would embrace the promise and calling on their lives. Pray that the eyes of their heart would be enlightened, and that they would know their Heavenly Father well."

"Thanks, Dave. I will do this."

"Chris, God has a lot to say about family. He tells us to love our wives, and He tells us not to exasperate our children.[xxxv] Exasperate means not to bug them. Don't major on the minors. So what if they dye their hair green and have a Mohawk haircut. Who cares? God says to nurture and admonish them; this takes time. You know that the Jewish people taught their children about the Lord when they walked along the road and when they laid down. They were encouraged by the Lord to invest personal, intimate time with their kids. Today we have made many mistakes in this area. We work long hours, and we don't see our kids much. We have five to ten minutes with them if we are lucky. You can't build a good relationship if you don't spend much time with them. It doesn't just happen.

"'Nurture' is a term a gardener uses to look after his garden. You nurture plants to produce a good crop by paying daily attention to them. You weed the garden, add fertilizer, and occasionally direct the plant for vines to grow the right way. You cannot force a vine, or you will break it. You have to gently pick up the vine and direct it in the right way by carefully wrapping it around the vine trellis you want it to grow on. So, it is with children. We have to admonish them to grow the right way. You have to direct them with gentleness. They can break.

"Admonishment takes time—time to listen, reason, and counsel—to help a young person to understand. Most of us fail in this area, but as I said at the start, don't be too hard on yourself. We all fail, and kids are quite resilient. They want a relationship with us. Ask forgiveness for your mistakes, and listen to them. You may have to earn the right to be heard again, but work at it, and you will accomplish what the Lord wants you to do."

"Thanks, Dave. I have to admit I have failed in these areas. I have been too harsh, too dogmatic, and I certainly have not listened enough. When the kids were growing up, I was always trying to figure out how to make a living, and it was tough. I did not make enough money, and every month we were in the red. It was a time of high stress."

"Chris, God knows how hard it was. Trust Him, and He will resolve these regrets you have." I felt tears coming to my eyes. "I love my kids, and I wish I had done a better job when I was raising them."

"Chris, don't be so hard on yourself. Kids don't come with an owner's manual. All parents have made mistakes. Kids are very resilient and forgiving. Just keep loving them and be humble. As they get older and have kids of their own, they will understand how tough the job was. You are your own hardest critic."

CHAPTER EIGHTEEN

Relationship

"**M**y wife is driving me crazy. If I knew that marriage was going to be like this, I would have never got married."

"Wow, Andrew, what is the matter?"

"Carol wants me to cut the grass, paint the house, go on a vacation, and buy a new car. The list never seems to end. She has a friend who lives in Orchard Heights, and she seems to have money coming out of her ears. Every time Carol comes home from her place, she has another list of things she wants. I can't take it anymore. I love Carol, but I cannot meet all these demands."

Andrew and Carol Matheson were both raised in Greenville. They got married in their last year at university. After living in the city for a couple of years, they moved back to Greenville to raise a family. Andrew was Sales Rep for a large industrial equipment company. Carol was an accountant. They bought a lovely house in a new housing development just south of town.

"Andrew, you know there is another thing in family relationships the Lord wants us to do."

"What is that?" asked Andrew.

"'Husbands, love your wives, just as Christ loved the church.'[xxxvi]

This type of love is very demanding. It means you lay down your desires for the sake of your wife. It means you love her like Christ loved the Church. He died for His Church. It requires tremendous self-sacrifice. Most men fail in this area. They expect their wives to submit and serve them."

"Chris, does it not say in the Bible, 'wives are to submit to their husbands'?"

"Andrew, if you examine the Scripture, it starts by saying, 'Submit to one another out of reverence for Christ,'[xxxvii] and then states, 'Wives, submit yourselves to your own husbands as you do to the Lord. For the husband is the head of the wife as Christ is the head of the church, his body, of which he is the Saviour. Now, as the church submits to Christ, so also wives should submit to their husbands in everything.'[xxxviii] Unfortunately, the word 'submit' in verses 22 through 24 is not in the original Greek text. Translators added these down through the ages. The result is there is an overemphasis on the responsibility of a woman to submit."

"Why did this happen?" inquired Andrew.

"Andrew, the Bible was translated by men, and I can't help wondering if there's a bit of male chauvinism involved. Verse 21 is the key verse, and it focuses on learning to submit to one another. The word 'submit' is a complicated word in Greek. It can undoubtedly mean to submit to a person's command or order, but it can also mean listening to each other's admonishment.

"I believe these three Scriptures tend to lean more towards that meaning because the only time the word 'submit' is used is in verse 21, and in that case, it is an operating principle for the Body of Christ. I believe we accomplish this when we listen to each other, when others give us advice and warnings, and when we are not so proud that we think we know everything."

"How come I have never heard this before?"

"Andrew, most people don't dig into what the original language says and just take things at face value. Also, many Christians never really read their Bible. They just listen to preachers who give their spin on a verse, leading to many errors and problems. The apostle Paul told Timothy a great truth that Dave told me very early in my walk with God. He said, 'Do your best to present yourself to God as one approved, a worker who does not need to be ashamed, and who correctly handles the word of truth.'

"When I learned this verse, I memorized it in the King James Version of the Bible, and the first word in that verse was 'study.' It has always stuck with me that I needed to study the Scriptures. As well as listen to God. Today studying the Bible has gone out of fashion, and as a result, we have some severe biblical literacy problems in the Church today.

"We need to learn humility, practice receiving instruction, and not take offense when corrected. This is a tough one."

"That's for sure," replied Andrew.

"All too often, as people rise in leadership, they become unteachable, especially if they are very gifted. The most dangerous person in the Body of Christ is a highly gifted but deeply wounded person. They are often very easily offended, don't take correction well, and cause many problems."

"Chris, Carol and I have always done our best to raise our kids well, but frankly, I often get very frustrated with them, and l lose my temper. Carol is the one who is the voice of reason. I feel at times that I am like a bottle. I stuff small irritants into the bottle, then put a cork in it. Over time the bottle gets full and, all of a sudden, the cork pops out, and I explode. I seem to be able to stay quiet and listen for the longest time, then all of a sudden, it becomes too much for me, and I boil over. This often happens when she talks to me about all the problems with the kids or her work. At some point, I can't take it anymore, and I want to act. I start to yell, and then I feel bad. It is so frustrating."

"Andrew, you are not alone. Most men struggle with this problem. Men and women are different. Women want to talk, and men want to act. Women need to speak; it is a crucial way they relieve stress. Men want to fix things. That's the way they relieve stress. If men think their wives are unhappy, men want to fix the situation; however, just because your wife is talking about something, it may not mean she wants you to fix it. She may just want you to listen to her. Your wife needs you to listen to her, serve your family, care for your children, and show kindness. She needs you to be a rock of stability.

"Consider all the things she has been telling you when she comes home from her Orchard Heights friends. She doesn't necessarily expect you to do all those things right away. She just needs to vent. She might be feeling a bit jealous or frustrated about her situation, and needs to vent. Remember, men want to fix things. We want to do all the items wives ask us. We want to please them. When your wife is venting, you think she wants these things all done, which builds up anxiety and frustration in you, and you blow your stack. It is pretty standard. The solution is to listen, acknowledge her requests, perhaps have her write down her desires, and put them on the fridge or in a job jar. Ask her, "Which one of these things would you like done first?" Then try to do the thing that is most important to her. She will be happy that something is getting done, and you will not feel like it is too much, because one request is manageable.

"I remember a family in our church a few years ago that had great kids, and I asked the father how he did it. He was the President of a company, and he had a very demanding role. He said, 'consistency.' I thought to myself, 'That is a tough thing to accomplish.' I have not achieved that in my life. I was often uptight and lost my temper when the kids were young. Our wives need us to be consistent, stable, dependable, and a tower of strength. They need us to serve our families.

"Remember what Jesus said to His disciples when they were arguing about who would be the greatest. He said, 'Whoever wants to become great among you must be your servant.'xxxix Servanthood starts with our family, with our wives and kids. We need to learn to serve them. They need us to participate in all the things within the house, from caring for the children, cooking, cleaning, paying the bills, and taking care of your property. Practical daily service is a key to a happy family.

"It used to be men would say, 'I don't do women's work,' and they would classify things like cooking, cleaning, and caring for children as women's work. This attitude is not serving your family. I'm glad to see that our new fathers understand that. This old behaviour and belief system is pretty well gone in new fathers. But many of our more senior church members and many who have recently immigrated still hold to this belief system.

"We are also responsible for protecting our wives and family. It may be an old concept in this society, but I suggest it is still very relevant. Protection today may not be the same as it was in the past. For example, we don't need to protect them from wild animals or something like that, but we need to protect them and our home from financial insolvency. Remember what Dave said about stewardship a couple of weeks ago? He talked about the need for us as men to provide for our family. That is the primary responsibility of a husband. It helps our family feel secure and protected.

"Andrew, we fathers are given a great deal to accomplish by the Lord, and we don't always do it well. However, there is forgiveness. Don't be hard on yourself. Just repent, and ask your Heavenly Father to help you do better, and He will."

"Thanks, Chris. I'll try to do this."

"Andrew, you don't have to do this all on your own. God will help you. Here is my most common prayer when it all seems too much: 'Dad help me.'"

Sometimes this is the most powerful prayer we can make.

CHAPTER NINETEEN

Press On

"I have decided to start a new practice. I'm going to start eating fruit and porridge. Please give me the Healthy Man's breakfast," said Jim.

The whole group was shocked. Here our faithful consumer of mass quantities of bacon, sausage, and everything fried had just changed his lifestyle. It was a reflection of our entire men's group. The last year had been a year of significant change for all of us. We were not the same men that we were a year ago.

"I realize that I was not a good steward of my body," said Jim. "I felt the Lord impress on me to lose weight and exercise. I have lost twenty pounds, and I'm walking every day. I am a new man."

We were all new in the way we were looking at life. Dave's message a year ago had changed our perspective. We no longer looked at ourselves and our little world in the same way. We were now looking at how we could be light in the world. David taught us to focus on accomplishing what Jesus wanted us to do, and as a result, our world was changing.

As a result of Jason's decision to go into politics, we had an influx of changes to our town. He converted our old downtown area into a trendy neighbourhood, and now coffee shops and restaurants have been opening up. Many of these businesses have been started by young people who have decided to stay in our town and start a business. The old glass factory reopened, a new company picked up the facility, and we can see a return of good jobs. I can't help but feel that Thomas and Caleb's reconciliation and repentance had changed our community's atmosphere. It is like Heaven has opened up over our little town. Paul's garage has expanded since he started the button jar program. It seems that when you sow generosity, you reap a harvest in kind. Our little town has changed.

Dave turned to us at the end of our breakfast and told us the best news. "You all know Cindy has been struggling with cancer this year. I am glad to report cancer has retreated. They thought they would have to take two-thirds of her liver, but when the surgeon got in there, he found the tumour had virtually disappeared, and he only ended up taking a few bits, about 10% of her liver. Today she is cancer-free."

The table exploded. Men were whistling, shouting, and praising God. The whole restaurant was in an uproar. Dave continued, "I never thought I'd see this day. I thought I would lose the love of my life, and yet my Heavenly Father showed Himself strong to me. Thank you for your prayers. My heart is full, and although my eyes are full of tears, they are tears of joy and thanksgiving."

The rest of the men also started to cry. They quickly wiped away the tears, but they could not hold back their emotions. Our Pastor had shown us he was as vulnerable as we are, and we could not contain our feelings.

"Men, I imagine that if in only one year we have seen this much change in our town and families by simply choosing each day to ask ourselves, 'What would Jesus want me to accomplish?' what could happen if we lived our entire lives this way? I think we could change the world." The room went quiet. What a thought—change the world. Dave continued, "Some disciples in Thessalonica were brought before their city Council with the charge that these men had turned the world upside down.[xl] The twelve disciples of Jesus changed the world as they knew it. I think we can do the same.

"The apostle Paul said, 'I press on to the goal [set before me].'xli He likened himself to an athlete, a long-distance runner who daily ran the race set before him. We need to do the same thing. To press on, and change our world one day at a time, one life at a time. Jesus told us, 'You are the light of the world.'xlii He challenged us to be that. I think we have made the first few steps towards accomplishing this."

We all agreed as we left the Cozy Corner restaurant. The world looked different. Instead of thinking about retirement and looking forward to a life of leisure, we began talking about how we could change the world.

Epilogue

C hanging the world starts with kindness, one act of generosity, one act of merely showing gratitude. It is not a significant project with thousands of carefully scheduled tasks. It is just the purposeful thought of individuals pressing forward, using their minds to consider how they can accomplish the things Jesus wants them to do. Each of us has the same challenge.

The men of Greenville Community Church changed their town, their church, and their own lives by merely responding to this challenge. A simple Pastor's message at a men's breakfast changed their town. If men and women embraced the same simple word, the result would be a movement that changes the world. Will you accept that challenge today? Will you make it your daily desire to accomplish what Jesus wants you to do, and demonstrate that you love the Lord your God with all your heart, soul, mind, and strength, and love your neighbour as yourself? I bless your journey.

Yours,
Chris Martin

GREENVILLE COMMUNITY CHURCH
MEN'S GROUP ATTENDEES

———— ∞∞ ————

NAME	PROFESSION
Dave and Cindy Williams	Pastors of Greenville Community Church
Mike and Sandra Brown	Mechanic at Greenville Auto
Chris and Linda Martin	Chris—consultant (author of the story)
	Linda—nurse
Richard and Nancy Brown	Farmers who employed Joseph and helped him develop his farming skills and immigrate to Greenville
Joseph and Maria Rodriguez	Farmer and landed immigrants from Mexico
Daniel and Sharon Miller	Friends of Mohammed and Zahra Abu
Paul and Michelle Robinson	Owner of Greenville Auto
Mark and Sarah King	Separated couple
Don and Angela Taylor	Cozy restaurant owners
Mohammed and Zahra Abu	Recent immigrants from Syria
Lawrence Lee & Gloria Wang	Investment broker
Thomas and Sandra Andrews	Retired shop steward at Clifford Glass
Caleb and Alexis Lewis	Former plant manager at Clifford Glass
Calvin and Joyce Kim	Convenience store owner
Jeff Masters	Retired corporate trainer
Jason Anderson	Teacher and town councilperson
Andrew and Carol Matheson	Young married couple
Jim Michaels	The quarterback of the football team forty years ago
Wesley Smith	Captain of the football team
Cliff Wallace	Widower

Endnotes

i   Matthew 28:19-20

ii   John 5:19

iii   Luke 10:1-24

iv   Mark 12:30

v   John 14:12-14

vi   Genesis 1:28

vii   I Timothy 2:1-2

viii   Matthew 20:26

ix   Proverbs 27:17

x   Luke 10:27

xi   Hebrews 10:25

xii   1 Corinthians 12:12-27

xiii   Mark 8:22-25

xiv   1 Corinthians 12:29

xv   2 Chronicles 7:14

xvi   2 Chronicles 7:14

xvii   Matthew 18:18

xviii   Ephesians 6:12, KJV

xix   Ezekiel 22:30

xx   Mark 1:15, KJV

xxi   Luke 17:21, KJV

xxii   Luke 11:20

xxiii   Joyce Meyer, *Battlefield of the Mind: Winning the Battle in Your Mind* (Tulsa, Oklahoma: Harrison House, 1995).

xxiv   Philippians 4:8, KJV

xxv   Hebrews 12:11

xxvi   Psalm 37:23, KJV

xxvii   John 11:35

xxviii   Matthew 12:10-13

xxix   Matthew 9:20-22

xxx   Luke 17:12-14

xxxi   I Timothy 5:8

xxxii   Proverbs 13:24

xxxiii   Joel 2:25

xxxiv   Romans 8:28

xxxv   Ephesians 6:4

xxxvi   Ephesians 5:25

xxxvii   Ephesians 5:21

xxxviii   Ephesians 5:22-24

xxxix   Mark 10:43

xl   Acts 17:6

xli   Philippians 3:14

xlii   Matthew 5:14

Author's Note

Early in my Christian walk, I read Charles Monroe Sheldon's book, *In His Steps*, a book about a church a hundred years ago which decided to ask themselves, "What would Jesus do?" before making any decision. They decided to do this after a tramp had come into the church and told them his story and died soon after. This book's practicality permanently moved me. It challenged people from all walks of life to examine their life, and a town was changed.

A few years ago, Sue and I wrote a book called *The Goal*. That book was an in-depth study of discipleship. I wrote the book *The Challenge* to transfer the content of *The Goal* into a story that would be easy for men to read—something quick that would impact other men the way Charles' book influenced me, and help others see practical ways to become a disciple of Christ today and change their world.

If you would like to learn about the eighty-three things that Jesus wants us to accomplish and how you can live in the kingdom of God, I recommend you read *The Goal*, or download the entire list from our website: www.thesecretplace.ca/resources.

I would love to hear your thoughts about this novel and how it impacted you. Feel free to email me at the.secret.place@cogeco.ca.

About the Author

William and Susan Dupley have been ministering for over thirty-five years, preaching and leading worship on five continents. Together they minister renewal and teach adults and children how to hear the voice of God. Bill and Sue believe that the supernatural should be natural for all believers and that every believer can impact their world for the kingdom of God as they hear God's will and follow His leading.

Bill and Sue's home church is the Freedom Centre in Oakville, Ontario, Canada. Together they have co-authored several books, including *Kids in Renewal*, a dynamic Sunday school program published by Strang Publishing that teaches children their Heavenly Father's heart for them, how to hear His voice, and how to receive and impart spiritual gifts. *The Secret Place* is a personal devotional that explains how to hear the voice of God and how to be fathered by your Heavenly Father. *The Goal: Be Light in the World* describes how to be light of the world in daily practical ways and how to make disciples.

Bill and Sue are certified facilitators for Communion with God Ministries and are affiliated with the Harvest Alliance. They have conducted seminars at Catch the Fire, Mission Fest, Releasers of Life,

Iris Ministries, and many other churches in North America, Africa, Australia, Europe, and Asia. Their passion is for God's family to know their Heavenly Father and to hear His voice so that they may live in the fullness of the gifts and the freedom that Jesus bought for them.

Susan is a graduate of the University of Toronto in Nursing Science, and Bill is a graduate of Ryerson University in Electronics Technology.

Bill and Sue came to the Lord in 1976. The Lord has guided them through business careers. They delight in their family that the Lord has blessed them with and enjoy having the time to follow what the Lord is showing them.

ADDITIONAL MATERIAL

These are additional books and resources by William and Susan Dupley that you may find helpful in your journey.

The Secret Place: The place to encounter revelations about your identity and your role in the kingdom of God and society. Author: William J. Dupley ISBN: 978-1-936860-01-2

The Goal: Be Light in the World. Authors William and Susan Dupley ISBN: 978-1-4600-0652-8

If you would like a complete list of the eighty-three things Jesus wants us to accomplish, download "Biblical references of what Jesus wants us to accomplish" from www.thesecretplace.ca/resources

If you would like to learn how to hear the voice of God and start journaling, download "How to Hear the Voice of God" from www.thesecretplace.ca/resources

ENDORSEMENTS

"Bill's books are always a joy to read: easy to read but a deep message. That isn't different for this book. Although it's written as a fiction book, it touched my heart. It encourages to go the extra mile, to become a world changer. I would encourage every Christian (new or Christian for many years) to get inspired by this book."

—Ilse Desaeger, Senior Pastor of Gloriepoort, a Catch The Fire Partner Church in Belgium

"Ever since the A-bomb, novelists and movies have offered us a variety of apocalyptic stories.

The Challenge takes us into almost unknown territory, exploring some of the possibilities for the common good that can spring from imaginative idealism. This is a 'What if?' story that prompts you to think, 'This could really happen!'"

—Rev. Al Reimers, Belleville, Ontario, Canada

"This book takes the Journey to greater faith and dependence on God in an insightful story of ever-increasing trust in God, and how the supernatural life of a Christ-follower is lived out. It is an interesting journey that leads us into that deeper relationship."

—Rev. Ken Raymer, Interim Lead Pastor, Listowel Pentecostal Church

"Life is a journey, and this journey is enriched as we walk it with others. It is enriched still more when we can truly make a difference in the lives of those around us. The longing of God's heart is that His people can bring His love and grace in all its beauty into the communities they live in, creating new stories and breakthroughs along the way. Bill's writing demonstrates his heart for this transformation, and paints a picture of what could happen as faith is stirred up in the Church."

—David Wuyts, former Pastor, Lifehouse Colchester, UK

"Jesus told stories to stab people awake to life-changing truth. This modern-day story packs a punch that has the power to wake up ordinary people to the fact that they can live extraordinary lives. Take up 'The Challenge!'"

—Fred Fulford, Professor Emeritus, Summit Pacific College

"I was first introduced to *The Challenge* by Bill over lunch one day when I mentioned our Men's Group at Singing Waters. We had been meeting for five years, and I knew that God was preparing a plan and a new purpose for us to come into. Reading this book has encouraged all of us to allow our Father to use our unique gifts and fellowship with each other, to not only impact our Ministry but also the Community. A wonderful read, full of great characters that bring real purpose and insights that challenge and encourage you to grow your faith!"

—Peter Leishman, Ministry Team, Singing Waters Ministries

"Everyone loves a story. To hear of other people's life experiences is an encouragement to us all. In *The Challenge*, Bill brings to life the simplicity of Evangelism as he breaks it down to a simple, 'What can I do?' Bill's books are enjoyable and easy to read, and *The Challenge* is no exception. He takes the reader on a journey of faith and anticipation, as all the characters in the book explore their individual gifts to bring light and life to their community. It is an inspiring book and a great encouragement to us all to ask ourselves, 'What can I accomplish?'"

—John and Pauline Arnott, Founding Pastors of Catch The Fire, Melbourne

"*The Challenge* makes you believe the 'impossible' is 'possible,' and that it can happen through everyday ordinary people like you and I. Personally, I found it to be really practical and down to earth at its heart. It was both encouraging and instructional throughout. Within its pages, there are little 'manna-bites' that feed and satisfy the soul's desire to be more like Jesus and to see Him made real in your own personal world.

An enjoyable weekend read that makes you hunger for the more that is available in God's Kingdom."

—**Kevin Cormier**

"A challenge happens when we arrive at the crossroads of decision. A wise person once said, 'It is in your moment of decision that your destiny is formed.' This book, *The Challenge*, is one of those crossroads. I believe God is speaking through His people to raise world changers for such a time as this. Who are these world changers? In days past, it was the Billy Grahams, Kathryn Kulmans, and Reinhard Bonnkes of the world. Today I believe it can be you and I. My entire life was transformed by a challenge. I challenge you to read and seriously consider the simplicity of *The Challenge* and ask yourself these five simple words as you read—'What can I do today?'"

—**Jason Shawera, Founder of The Joshua 1:9 Academy**

"I very much enjoyed reading *The Challenge*, and I found it very helpful. I appreciated the easy-to-read structure of the book, the relatable characters, and the realistic situations presented. The theme of how to accomplish living as Jesus commanded, offers practical lessons through how the novel's characters managed the situations they were faced with. Their stories of how they managed, taught me how to have a closer personal relationship with God the Father, and how to take practical steps to practice what Jesus taught.

I really did enjoy the book, Bill. I found myself wishing that I could be a part of the Greenville Community, and I could relate to the situational challenges they experienced. Good work, Bill."

—**Dan Davis, MSW (retired)**

CPSIA information can be obtained
at www.ICGtesting.com
Printed in the USA
BVHW040439130821
613491BV00004B/11